Oshkosh Remembered

Ron La Point

Copyright © 2024 Ron La Point

All rights reserved. No part of this book may be reproduced or transmitted in any form or by any means, electronic or mechanical, including photocopying, recording or by any information storage and retrieval system without permission in writing from the publisher.

Ron La Point—Oshkosh, WI
ISBN: 979-8-8693-3094-9
Title: *Oshkosh Remembered*
Author: Ron La Point
Digital distribution | 2024
Paperback | 2024

Dedication

I would like to dedicate the book: Oshkosh Remembered, to Dan Radig, an Oshkosh historian whose countless collection of old Oshkosh photographs that aided me in illustrating stories, not only in this book, but in each of my other Oshkosh books as well. Without Dan's efforts and the many hours he and I have spent together, the books would not have been the same.

Table of Contents

Introduction vii
Foreword ix
Chapter One: Wood and Lumber Industry 1
Chapter Two: Paine Lumber Company and the
                Woodworker's Strike of 1898 13
Chapter Three: German Immigration 22
Chapter Four: Women's Suffrage 31
Chapter Five: Racial Segregation 37
Chapter Six: Prohibition 45
Chapter Seven: The Great Depression 56
Chapter Eight: Aviation 65
Chapter Nine: Athearn Hotel 72
Chapter Ten: Movie Theaters 84
Chapter Eleven: Stein's Department Store 92
Chapter Twelve: Taverns 102
Chapter Thirteen: Fishing Shanties 113
Chapter Fourteen: World War II 122
Chapter Fifteen: Grocery Stores 133
Chapter Sixteen: EWECO Park 139
Chapter Seventeen: Oshkosh All Stars 146
Chapter Eighteen: Baseball 155
Chapter Nineteen: Bowling 167
Chapter Twenty: Lakeshore Golf Course 175
Chapter Twenty-One: Polio 181
Chapter Twenty-Two: Highway 41 186
Chapter Twenty-Three: The New Immigrants 193
Chapter Twenty-Four: Donnie Weitz 209
About the Author 220

Introduction

I was recently asked by a women's book club to talk about *Women of Oshkosh*, a book I had recently written. The book included twenty-seven women who played major roles in advancing and improving our community.

After passing a list of those I included in the book to each of the members present, I talked about three who lived during the early part of the 20th century and one who wrote about that part of our history.

After a short presentation many in attendance asked what life was like for those living in Oshkosh during this time. I managed to answer a few, but only a few, and then only partially. I was both surprised and pleased with the interest that was shown, but also disappointed that I was unable to provide a clearer picture of our city's past.

The reason I've been writing books about the history and people of Oshkosh is to contribute a fuller understanding of our local history. Much of my writing is based on personal interviews, although I also explore books and articles that help me understand both the event and the developing story. And the experiences and information I gathered while living in Oshkosh for 80-plus years helps as well.

This book, I believe, helps us better understand and appreciate our city's past. I am including stories of events and other happenings that have taken place between the turn of the century and the 1950s, although a few of these stories had their beginnings some years earlier.

But it's not only events that have shaped our past. Without

the likes of Hank Dettlaff, Frank Stein, Steve Wittman, Lonnie Darling, "Inky" Jungwirth and a host of others, our history would not be the same or as meaningful.

Those familiar with my writings will notice that some of these stories or parts of them have been included in some of my other books. But much of the book is based on additional interviews and exploring related sources.

I am not suggesting that this should be a primary source to understand the history of Oshkosh. It is not. I'm not an Oshkosh historian. I simply write about our city's past and its people hoping to contribute an appreciation of events that have helped shape our city.

It is my hope that reading these stories offers each of us an opportunity to reflect and to wonder whether the events of the past helps us understand the city we live in today.

Foreword

This is quite an honor to write the foreword for Ron La Point's latest book. Like Ron, I'm an Oshkosh native who deviated from Oshkosh residency briefly before coming back home after getting my education. I've enjoyed remembrances of former Oshkosh residents some of which I knew some that I'd heard of, and others whose stories were new to me.

My acquaintance with Ron goes back to the 1967-68 school year at Oshkosh High when Ron arrived as a history teacher and debate coach. I was a student in both capacities. I reestablished the acquaintance when Ron took a gig as a bailiff in the Winnebago County Courthouse after his retirement. We've chatted regularly as he hawked his books at the Oshkosh Farmers Market.

In this book Ron continues his Oshkosh stories in style similar to prior books including, "Oshkosh: A South Sider Remembers" (2008), "Oshkosh: The Way We Were" (2010), "Oshkosh: Preserving The Past" (2012), "Oshkosh: Its History, Its People" (2015), "Oshkosh: Looking Back" (2019), "Women of Oshkosh" (2021) and "Oshkosh Veterans of Foreign Wars" (2023). Some of the topics that are covered in the prior books reappear in this book.

The book covers work and play in Oshkosh as well as social issues.

The work portion covers wood and the lumber industry, a separate story on the 1898 woodworker's strike, Paine Lumber and German immigration and the new immigrants to staff the industries in Oshkosh.

The play sections cover movie theaters, fishing shanties, Oshkosh All Stars, EWECO Park, Lakeshore Golf Course, baseball and bowling.

Other topics include social issues and events. Oshkosh was part of national and world events and Ron covered the angle on big issues like women's suffrage and prohibition. (Some say the two are related as the latter was not attained until the former). Local angles on the Great Depression, World War II and racial segregation are also covered. Oshkosh's stand as a sundown city and high tide of the Ku Klux Klan in Oshkosh are also covered.

There are also topics affecting commerce in Oshkosh. The bygone era when each neighborhood had a grocery store is remembered. A section covers select taverns of Oshkosh. The elegance of the Athearn Hotel which was razed in the 1960s and the elegance of Stein's Department Store lost to fire in the 1940s are remembered. Both had a reputation that exceeded the Oshkosh footprint.

This is a book that adds to the understanding of the social history of Oshkosh through the memories of those that lived it. It is a fascinating opportunity to peer into the local past with numerous one-of-a kind interviews. I think you will enjoy it.

Thomas J. King

Chapter One
Wood and lumber industry

*T*he names of Paine, Sawyer, Radford, Morgan, Buckstaff and a host of other lumber barons still resonate in Oshkosh, a place that was known far and wide as "Sawdust City."

Even during the 1950s and '60s, more than one hundred years after the first saw mill was built, there were still a number of wood manufacturers hugging the Fox River. Paine's, Badger Lumber, Foster Lothman's, Morgan's, Diamond Match, American Excelsior, Pluswood, Radford's and Buckstaff's come to mind. None of those remain today.

Some of their buildings still stand although most have been replaced with commercial and public developments. For instance, the largest of these companies was Paine's which was converted into a condominium complex in the early 1980s.

The Badger Lumber Company, on the south side of the river that manufactured Dearborn furniture, survived into the 1980s. The North Senior Center now occupies some of the building that housed the furniture company although much of the manufacturing part of the building is no longer there.

American Excelsior, located next to the Badger Lumber Company, with its towering piles of logs standing where the soccer field is now located next to the Fox Valley Technical College, is now the business district on the southeast side of the Wisconsin Avenue Bridge.

Foster Lothman was located on the river north of 6th and Minnesota streets. The building was razed many years ago. There was also a large, flat fishing dock next to the factory where many fishermen cast their lines. There was an incident there that is still remembered by many in this city. For whatever reason, a car was being driven north on Minnesota Street onto the dock without slowing down and plunged into the river. The car was later recovered. I'm not sure about the driver.

Morgans with its tramway connecting its two major buildings on 6th and Oregon streets, and its other buildings along the Fox River were fully demolished in 2014. Their property still stands empty today.

Diamond Match, a large building known throughout the country for manufacturing matches was razed in the 1970s and is now a part of the University.

Pluswood Industries, located on the corner of Sawyer and Oshkosh avenues has been converted into a park.

Radford's, located on the north side of the river north to Pearl Street is now called the Radford Square Mini Mall. One of Radford's last buildings razed was used as a temporary library in the early 1990s when improvements were being made to the Oshkosh Public Library.

Buckstaff's, the last of the lumber companies is now the home of the Oshkosh Arena.

The largest of these companies were Paine's, Morgan's, Radford's and Buckstaff's. I'm including stories only about Radford's, Morgan's and Buckstaff's despite Paine's being the largest and most profitable of the lumber mills. Paine's is covered in another story in the book.

Oshkosh would not be the city it is today without the lumber industry's impact in the area. The industry would go on to become one of the primary forces of growth and development in the Winnebago County area. The city's location on Lake Winnebago and nearby waterways made it the ideal place for it later being known as the "Sawdust Capital of the World."

The Oshkosh lumber industry was spurred by the string of water ways that flowed into the city. The Wolf River, in its upper reaches that contain vast forests of northern pines, flows south into a chain of lakes – Poygan, Winneconne and Butte des Mort – then enters the Fox River with its collection of logs used to make wood products.

Logs on the Fox River

The arrival of the railroad and the great Chicago fire in 1871 created a boom in Oshkosh lumber trade. Much of the lumber used to rebuild Chicago was produced by Oshkosh sawmills.

Men living in the east had heard of the wonderful tales of wealth made easy at Oshkosh. Sawdust City became a mecca for hundreds of laborers, some without a cent in the world, others with a small accumulation obtained in the east. They all came to Oshkosh, some invested their time and money, others their time only.

The Radford name in Oshkosh is almost as old as the city. The September 16, 1905 issue of the *Weekly Northwestern* helps to tell their story.

It was on one bright morning on October 3, 1855 about ten o'clock, that a river steamer pulled up to a dock near the mouth of the river. A young man, sprightly and with an air of business about him that attracted attention at once, jumped down the gang plank with a bundle slung over his shoulder. This bundle contained all his worldly possessions. In his pocket a lone ten cent piece jingled lonesomely against a large jack knife. It was all the money he had in the world.

The young man, after asking a few questions of bystanders, walked up the river bank and soon arrived at a mill and made an application for work. "What is your name?" was asked. "William Radford of New York," was the ready reply.

Radford soon went to work at 6 o'clock in the evening of the same day for the firm of Ripley, Mean & Chase and for one month continued in his position. After his one month was up, D.L. Libbey, a former well-known lumberman of the city, now deceased, bought out the shares controlled by Ripley and Mead. Mr. Radford was named the head sawyer of this circular mill and retained that position for the next three years.

From that time on he continued to rise until at the present day, he, with his son, Charles W. Radford and brother, Stephen Radford, conducted one of the largest planning and saw mills in the northwest. The first of next October will mark the 50th anniversary of William Radford's engagement in the lumber business in Oshkosh. He is considered the oldest man in the business today in Oshkosh and there is not another known case in the northwest where one man has successfully conducted a saw mill business for fifty consecutive years in any one place. It is believed that William Radford enjoys that distinction alone.

The *Oshkosh Northwestern* of July 27, 1972 continues with the story of the Radfords.

Bill Radford purchased the Libbey sawmill with his brother Stephen in 1871. The Radford Company sash and door mill prospered under their leadership. Today, Radford's great grandson, Charles M. Radford is president and general manager of Radford Company, a firm which presently is a wholesale distributer of millwork products.

As a whole sale distributor, Radford Company buys millwork such as doors, windows, window frames and moldings from manufacturers and assembles the parts. The company then sells the building materials to contractors and lumber dealers.

The company also does a limited amount of specialized woodworking such as replacing windows for older houses. According to Charles Radford the company is one of the few millwork concerns remaining which will take individual customer's woodworking job orders.

The original Radford plant was located on the site of the old Pipkorn building next to the Wisconsin Avenue Bridge on the north side of the river. When the company remodeled in the late 1960s, excavators unearthed an old plank road eight feet below the present sea level.

It had been determined earlier that the accumulation of sawdust, slabs and other refuse from logs used by lumber companies, could be used as a fill-in on the low land abutting the Fox River, and, as a result, new saw mills sprang up in quick succession.

Charles Radford attributed the eight foot rise in elevation to the sawdust pile landfill, accumulated over the years. Part of the original Radford Brothers plant sat under the present Wisconsin Avenue Bridge, Radford said. Sawdust piles built the land up to its present height.

One of the many lumber firms that grew up with the city is the Morgan Company. Its history stretches back into the era when Oshkosh came into prominence as the "lumber Capital of the World."

The Morgan Company manufactured doors, stairways, kitchen cabinets and a variety of other wood products that were sold throughout the country. Their first plants were destroyed by fire in the mid to late 1800s as were other businesses on the north side of the river. Their new factory was built in 1897.

In a June 9, 2009 column in the *Oshkosh Northwestern*, Patricia Wolf writes:

The closing of the Jen-Wen plant in August will not only mark the beginning of unemployment for 79 workers, it will also mark the final end of Oshkosh's once dominant and storied lumber industry that defined its first 100 years. "In my mind this closing would be the last gasp of the lumber era in the city of Oshkosh," said Clarence "Inky" Jungwirth, a local amateur historian.

The former Morgan Door Company, which occupied a large parcel of land along the Fox River at Oregon Street and Sixth Avenue had an overhead walkway connecting these two main buildings. This location was opened in 1868 by brothers Richard Thomas Morgan and John Rodgers Morgan.

The brothers had been involved in various partnerships for the manufacture of sashes, doors and blinds. They formed Morgan and Brothers in 1868 and became Oshkosh Morgan Brothers and Company after 1882 when a cousin Thomas Rowland Morgan joined according to the Wisconsin Historical Society.

Throughout the years Morgan's gained a reputation as the maker of fine wood products including doors, windows, fireplace mantels and stair railings. Next to the Paine Lumber Company, it was the largest lumber company in the city. At its height, they employed around 1,000 workers according to Jungwirth.

Jeld-Wen, based in Klamath Falls, Oregon bought the former Morgan Door Company in 1998. At the time Morgan's still employed 373 people.

Marv Schwebke, who first started work for Morgan's in 1948, stayed with the company until 1990 as a grinder and a molding sticker making stair rail parts, and said he saw the end coming even back then.

"I loved the work. I loved the people," Schwebke said. "Everything was teamwork. I could see it coming when I retired. Things were going downhill in the attitude. There was no teamwork."

Employees were notified Friday about the August 7 closing. The Oshkosh plant was the company's last to manufacture solid wood and rail doors. At the time there were 79 employees.

The headline in the *Oshkosh Northwestern of December 8,2021* reads: Former Morgan Door Site in Oshkosh sold to new developer.

A prime strip of riverfront property in downtown Oshkosh is under new ownership. The former Morgan Door Company site has been sold to a firm in Ohio. A group of local developers called the Morgan Group initially purchased the site in 2016 with plans for a multi-purpose development including apartments and retail. Nothing was ever built on the property. A real estate broker representing the new owners will only say that the proposed development will not be residential or industrial – and an announcement on the plans will be made early next year. The purchase price has not been disclosed. The city has allowed approved tax incremental financing incentives for that site.

Terry Laib, a member of the National Trust Preservation Society, is in business to restore historic buildings had this to say about the Morgan building some years ago during one of our interviews.

"The Morgan Door factory is another example of lost history for Oshkosh. I was interested in the property. Had it come my way I had planned to restore all of its buildings including the two larger ones connected by the tramway overlooking Oregon Street a little north of Sixth. What I had in mind was making the first floor of the buildings retail and the second floor into apartments. I never had a chance to implement that plan."

"Jeld-Wen owned the property at the time. The city had given them a demolition permit that should not have been given. There's a city preservation ordinance that requires a 90 day waiting period before the owner can demolish their building."

"There is a good reason the waiting period is there. It allows for any interested person or persons to appear before the Planning Committee with other ideas regarding the use of the property. This was not done. The commission knew about the ordinance because I called the principal planner shortly after this occurred and he indicated that they did."

Morgan's Tramway Overlooking Oregon Street

Oshkosh wasn't yet a city when John Buckstaff arrived in 1850 and found a site on the riverfront community's south side and started his lumber business.

For the next 157 years, five generations of John A.

Buckstaff's family would own and operate the business in Oshkosh.

The following story, written by Jeff Bollier, appeared on the *Oshkosh Northwestern* on July 8, 2012

After more than 170 years the legacy of Buckstaff Lumber Company lives beyond its hand-crafted, solid wood furnishings that remain in several Oshkosh schools and businesses and throughout the United States to this day.

Bookshelves, tables and chairs still remain in most Oshkosh Area School District buildings as well as current and former restaurants such as the Roxy, Primo's and Red's Pizza and as far as Walt Disney world and the Pentagon.

Starting as a manufacture of coffins during the Civil War, Buckstaff evolved to ammo boxes in World War II and eventually what it is known for today: furniture.

The company that produced shingles, chairs, tables, ottomans, rockers, high chairs, desks, work benches and caskets of a quality, second to none, would last 161 years before unpaid bills and a mortgage foreclosure ended the company on February 16, 2011.

John Anderson, who worked at Buckstaff for forty-one years and a company historian, accumulated newspaper articles, historic information, photographs of all descriptions and additional memorabilia of Buckstaff since its inception. Much of what you read is due to this collection.

John, who graduated from the Fox Valley Technical School in Oshkosh with an Associated Degree in Conservation was hired by Buckstaff to run their dry kiln operation.

"I had a pretty good background in the lumber industry from my schooling and from my part-time work at the Paine

Lumber Company so I was comfortable doing the assigned work."

"When hired, I was told that I would be in a management position and would eventually run the entire lumber yard; the saw mill, the lumber stacker, and the dry kilns. I was asked to be the purchasing manager of the plant some years later after acquainting myself with the entire operation."

At that time he was part of the management team that met once a month to go over business functions, the company's outlook and its future.

"You could begin to tell when the new owner took over in 2007 that the company, now called Oshkosh Industries, was not doing as well as the company did earlier, much of it due to the changes he (Martin Cowie) made."

Jeff Bollier continues:

The family took great pride in winning several prominent contracts in the 1950s and '60s. The company provided more than 7,000 chairs for the Pentagon's dining hall in 1958. A U.S. Naval base in Virginia was outfitted with Buckstaff furniture, and the West Point cafeteria and library both contain Buckstaff items.

"John D. Buckstaff Jr. was always concerned about the quality of the product," former Buckstaff salesman Tom Mugerauer said. "He didn't want to send out anything that might come back. He took a lot of pride and putting the best product out there. And you can still see our product at restaurants, schools and libraries around town. Some of our chairs are 50 years old now and haven't been replaced."

Kirsten Buckstaff, the daughter of John D. Buckstaff Jr., said one of her most prized company possessions is a Victorian rocker or lawyer's chair she found at an estate sale in Florida some time ago. It came from an era in the 1880s when a new company began manufacturing chairs and caskets. It still contains the Buckstaff emblem embossed in leather on the back of the chair. She said she regularly scours eBay and Craigslist in search of company products.

"What survives from that era, we're lucky to find," she said. "Our family may have kept it quiet, but we produced products of exceptional quality, the kind of quality you can't really find anymore."

In a city that's had its share of internationally recognized lumber companies, Buckstaff was around longer than Oshkosh B'Gosh, Morgan Door or Leach Company.

Mugerarauer said the company remained profitable through downturns in the 1970s and '80s and was growing in the 1990s and early 2000s before changes in manufacturing and the global economy took their toll. But, he said, it wasn't the economy or costs that bought a 161 year history to an end. It was the amount the 161-year-old company's only non-family owner, Martin Cowie, owed Citizens Bank by the time the bank's foreclosure case came to a conclusion on June 6, 2011."

"Cowie borrowed almost $2 million from the bank from May 23, 2007, the day he purchased the business for $1,075,000 on February 15, 2008. He bought the company with a firm belief that he could re-energize it. In fact he told the *Northwestern* at the time that his goal was to triple Buckstaff's sales in three years. But the plan quickly unraveled as the bills mounted, suppliers stopped delivering and orders went unfilled."

"The name was pretty much trashed by that last year," Mugerauer said. "Orders went unfilled, bills went unpaid, deposits for orders we couldn't complete weren't returned, and salaries went unpaid. You couldn't make anything because the raw materials wouldn't be delivered. We couldn't ship anything because the trucking companies couldn't pick up an order. It became stressful."

John Anderson remembers that day on February 16, 2011 when several Public Service vehicles arrived and turned off the power grid. "Everyone went home wondering what was next for Buckstaff."

In 2016, the company's factory was demolished to pave the way for what's now the Oshkosh Arena, and as part of the city's continued work in the Sawdust district.

Chapter Two
Paine Lumber Company and the Woodworker's Strike of 1898

At the end of the 19th century, Oshkosh, with a population of 28,000, was one of the leading lumber centers in the country. It had long been known as the "Sawdust City" and was dominated economically by eight large companies that manufactured doors, blinds, window sashes and custom millwork. The Paine Lumber Company was the largest that included Radford, Morgan, Buckstaffs, McMillen, Williamson-Libbey, Foster Hafner (later to become Foster Lothman that most in my generation remembered) and Gould together employed about 2,000 woodworkers in their factories and yards.

This story is about George Paine and the Paine Lumber Company and reveals what life was like for the city's working class at the turn of the 20th century.

The information for this story was taking from Virginia Crane's book: "Oshkosh Woodworker's Strike of 1898: A Wisconsin Community in Crisis," and from a variety of other sources.

The workers employed at these large lumber companies in Oshkosh were mostly German immigrants. Their homes were concentrated on the city's south side. In that working-class community of modest frame houses on unpaved streets, these German residents were either Prussian Lutherans, namely those attending First English and Peace Lutheran churches, and Bohemian Catholic neighborhoods in the Sacred Heart Parish. The mill owners – English-speaking Presbyterians and Methodists – lived a world away, north of the river in finely crafted Victorian houses set along paved streets.

At the time and even years later, industrialists strongly resisted unions as threats to capitalist control of the workplace and the market. Governments at every level were controlled or shaped by big business. And, for the most part, merchants and the middle class associated unions with anarchism and violence.

In Oshkosh, as elsewhere, the rich stood out in glaring contrast to the poor. By a long-standing tradition, the city was seen as being divided by geography with the Fox River as the separation line dividing the upper class north side from the working class south side.

In 1898 George Paine of the Paine Lumber Company was the corporate monarch of Oshkosh. He dominated the city's millwork industry and employed over 750 workers – about a third of the city total. He was 65 years old, distinguished looking, dignified and austere. Like many an industrialist of the Gilded Age, Paine was a tight-fisted conservative who favored trusts and monopoly capitalism, feared anarchists and socialists, hated labor unions, and regarded his employees as objects of contempt. He considered laborers to be objects and not people.

Throughout the 1890s he and other local lumber company executives imported cheap foreign labor, repeatedly cut wages and hired women and children for half the pay that men received. Wages in the local millwork industry were so low – about ninety cents for ten hour day - that the *International Labor Press* referred to Oshkosh as the "slave wage capital of the world."

By 1898 the workers were ready to demand an improvement in working conditions and pay. When the mill owners ignored their efforts to increase wages, they decided they only way to improve their lot was to affiliate with the American Federation of Labor. They turned for help to Thomas Kidd, General Secretary of the AFL's International Machine Woodworker's Union located in Chicago.

Paine's woodworking factory

Kidd selected Oshkosh as his destination because from talks with members all over the country, he had come to realize that woodworkers in Oshkosh had the lowest wages of any woodworking center in the United States.

The union drafted a list of terms that included a 25% pay increase with a minimum of $1.50 a day, an end to the employment of women, recognition of the union, and regular weekly pay days. Although there was a law that said workers were to be paid weekly, the mill owners ignored it and it was not enforced.

The mill owners met to discuss the demands but failed to act. That Monday, May 16, the workers went on strike. Thirteen hundred workers stayed home that day but the mills continued to operate with small crews.

The strike continued for the week without incident. The next week Samuel Gompers, the head of the American Federation of Labor, arrived and spoke to the strikers. He said that the AFL would do whatever was needed to help the strikers. He said that the conditions and wages of the workers here were some of the worst he had ever seen. The strikers were rejuvenated after his visit and more strikers went on picket duty.

After the strike had gone on for more than three weeks with no break in sight, George Paine and his cohorts and agents developed an aggressive new strategy to end the walkout on their own terms. The mayor, the police, the courts, private detectives and propaganda in the *Oshkosh Northwestern* were the instruments chosen to turn public opinion against the strikers, disrupt the picket system and the strike and destroy the unions.

With the strikers and Thomas Kidd under intense surveillance and in constant danger for false arrest, the women of the woodworker's families took over. At some point before June 22, dozens of wives and mothers of union workers organized themselves for action on behalf of their men and in opposition to the scabs who were keeping the seven mills operating.

Pickets outside the gates at opening and closing times took down the names of workers and tried to influence them not to go into the mill. When that didn't work, women, supporting their husbands and fathers, shouted threats and threw eggs and stones and clubbed the strikebreakers with three and four foot long boards when they entered and exited the mills. Workers soon grew afraid to show up and the mill closed because the crew at work was not large enough to operate the machinery resulting in heavy company losses.

When there was additional violence the National Guard was called in. They set up positions at the Morgan plant with Gatling guns. There was no violence after that.

When the clash between the owners and workers had lasted longer than most expected, the Oshkosh middle class began supporting the strikers as they began to consider it a class issue. The *Oshkosh enterprise* and the *Oshkosh Times* wrote editorials in support of the laboring class wanting a better life. Small retail merchants let credit accounts run up and local farmers contributed food to the striking families. When the union solicited merchants in town to ask donations for the poorest families of men out of work, a great many provided assistance.

By his nature, George Paine was incapable of dealing with direct challenges, to the "rightness" of his positions. His obsessive fear and hatred of unions made him unable to meet with a delegation that had union associations or when women asked to meet with him as his patriarchal culture did not suit him for dealing with outspoken women. His ruling class ideals required that he treat working people as inferiors.

On Friday, August 12 the Oshkosh Woodworker's union was ready to give up because they thought the mill owners would never compromise and the strike would never be won. It had accomplished the purpose of calling public attention to conditions in the millwork factories of the city. More importantly, the mill owners, by paying individual strikers who returned to work at the wage scale demanded by the union, had in effect admitted that some of their employees should have higher wages.

Many of the men left the city to take jobs elsewhere. Some men went to work in neighboring communities and some others went to work at another sash and door factory in Muscatine, Iowa. Some of these jobs were paying twice as much as the Oshkosh woodworking jobs.

Paine wanted those responsible for shutting down his company to be tried for criminal conspiracy. An indictment demanded by Paine and issued by the District Attorney stated that Thomas Kidd along with George Zentner and Michael

Troiber, two Oshkosh strikers, were scheduled to appear in the Oshkosh municipal court on Saturday, October 1 for the alleged crimes.

It was alleged that Thomas Kidd had incited the riots along the picket lines and had arranged for those picketing the mills to harass the strikebreakers to prevent them from working. George Paine testified that only 82 of the 600 or so employees of his company showed up for work because of the harassment.

Clarence Darrow, a friend and neighbor of Thomas Kidd and a well-known Chicago lawyer, decided to be the council for each of the defendants. He introduced his remarks at the trial by explaining that he became involved because of the workers struggle against oppression and tyranny and the promises of the United States Constitution.

Clarence Darrow, who would later become famous for his involvement in the Scopes "Monkey" trial in 1925, was scheduled to deliver the final defense summation on Monday, October 31. Early that morning, a capacity crowd waited at the courtroom door to hear the famous lawyer who had become well known to all of Oshkosh during the past several weeks. Darrow was a celebrity and was performing free of charge, and that brought out not only the merely curious but those interested in the case. Darrow was about to make the most famous speech in Oshkosh history.

Clarence Darrow

Darrow's involvement to the cause of freedom for industrial workers had made him a passionate advocate. The cause before him was dear to his heart. His sympathy had been aroused by what he perceived in Oshkosh as one of the darkest plots for the enslavement of men that he had ever seen.

Darrow said the verdict in the case would be a milestone in the history of the world. The issue was whether workers in America would be jailed for striking to better their conditions. If the three defendants in this historic case were sent to jail, there would never be another strike. It had fallen to the jury to play a leading role in one of the great dramas of human life.

During the second ballot the jury cast a unanimous vote for acquittal. The whole proceeding took about forty minutes.

But the decision did not stop Paine from continuing to recruit cheap labor and ignoring union activity. A few years after the trial, Oshkosh's ethnic history was reshaped when a new and cheaper labor force recruited by George Paine. They were Volga Germans from Russia.

George Paine died in 1917 and his son Nathan took over the company. In 1925 Nathan Paine built a block of row houses on Summit Avenue near the mill to provide apartments for his workers. The new housing was later called the Paine Flats.

The same year he organized a Paine Thrift Bank across the street from the mill and manipulated or coerced the workers into depositing their savings there.

During this time Nathan Paine and his wife started building an elegant mansion on Algoma Boulevard. The Panic of 1929 and the depression that followed caused the Paine bank to fail and many depositors lost their savings.

A number of workers in the 1930s who lost their savings, had relatives and friends who remembered Nathan Paine's role in the Woodworkers Strike of 1898. The heritage of hate that lingered from that experience with the Paine's seemed to have revived with the hard times of the depression years and rumors began to circulate the Paine Mansion would be bombed if Nathan Paine family ever moved in.

The mansion was soon donated to the city as an art museum and Oshkosh thus benefited culturally from the philanthropy of the family that had not been famous in 1898 for its generosity and charity.

To further illustrate how contemporaries of Nathan Paine felt, I'm including a short story from one of my former teachers, Lorraine Oaks Weiner. Her father was George Oaks, the former mayor of Oshkosh.

"This is one story about my dad I'll always remember. This incident in question was so typical of him."

"My dad loved flowers. So one day I took him to see the gardens in the Paine Arboretum. Before we had the chance to view the gardens it started to rain so we went inside. A very dignified docent met us and immediately took the two of us to a portrait of Nathan Paine. With hand over her heart, she said: 'And this is Nathan Paine.' 'Yeah I knew him.' The lady being very impressed asked 'What kind of man was he? Without hesitation Dad said 'He was a son of a bitch.' The lady gasped and fled. That was so much like Dad. He was outspoken and often stepped – mostly stomped – on toes of those he did not respect."

Chapter Three
German Immigration

German-speaking immigrants helped settle and build the city of Oshkosh. They came in three waves; from the rural Prussian province of Pomerania on the Baltic Sea; from villages along the border between Bavaria and Bohemia, which at the time was part of the Austro-Hungarian Empire during the 1850s, and later from German settlements along Russia's Volga River around 1900.

While they were all Germans to those residing in the city, there were large differences among them. They came from different countries, spoke different dialects, went to different churches, brought different traditions, and often did not agree with each other.

Those who arrived and settled on the city's south side were primarily the immigrants from Bavaria and Bohemia who became known as "Hi-Holders."

These German-speaking immigrants played a large role in the city's woodworking industry, and founded the many breweries, stores and taverns that have characterized our city's culture.

New residents to Oshkosh will occasionally hear older residents of the city talk about the Hi-Holders who lived on the south side of the river at the turn of the century. They frequently ask how the residents of this far south side area got its name.

In the early years the south side of the Fox River was the area where many Lutheran and Catholic Germans settled that emigrated from Bavaria and Bohemia. They came to work in the lumber mills located on both sides of the river. Many of the early German Catholic immigrants had barns on their property where a cow was kept for milking. In order to feed the cows, the families would take their wheelbarrows to the fields of hay located on the present-day site of South Park. They would cut the hay and bring it back to their homes.

In the late 19th and early 20th century the early Yankee settlers in the eastern part of the country had a strong dislike for new immigrants from Europe, especially those who were Catholic. This was true for the earlier settlers in Oshkosh as well. Many Oshkosh residents, especially those residing north of the river, looked down on the residents of the 6th Ward as second class citizens. It is said that eventually the term Hay Haulers degenerated into the term Hi-Holder as a negative version of the German word Hoi-Hauler.

Those German immigrants arriving from Pomerania were known as Plattdeutschers" or "Low Germans." Plattdeutscher clearly refers to the dialect of the German coastal areas that the Pomeranians spoke. The early Pomeranians tended to settled on both sides of the city. Those that came later settled on the north side primarily in a district called Nordheim, then outside the city limits. In 1950 Nordheim was annexed and became part of the city proper.

An *Oshkosh Northwestern* article of June 6, 1968 talks about these two distinctly different German immigrants.

The kids hollered "my dad can lick your dad" in German dialect during the old days on the south side. The "highholders" and the "lowlanders" feuded regularly and the two sides decided to organize a huge boxing match on Oregon Street every year to determine who was toughest.

The street was blocked off for the fight which became sort of an annual tradition even occurring in the 1940s and early '50s. Adding to the mix, one side was predominantly Lutheran, the other Catholic.

Only the census takers dared lump together all of Oshkoshians of German descent which comprised more than a third of the local population. Immigrants themselves nursed the same distinctive dialect and customs that separated feudal areas in the homeland. Bohemians, one of the largest local segments, mistrusted the Plattdeutschers in much the same way the Scots viewed the English in Great Britain.

The Bohemians were considered Germanic, though Austria ruled their native land. The term Highholders may also have referred to their origins in the highlands of the Bohmerwald forests. It was natural for the Bohemians, who were foresters in Europe, to settle in Oshkosh, the hub of the vast logging industry.

Plattdeutschers was the name which the Highholders gave to the immigrants from the lowlands and valleys of Germany. It meant "low Germans" and implied a lower social class. Plattdeutschers on the south side of Oshkosh lived to the area east of Ohio Street between 6th and 18th. There was also a sizeable German community on the north side in the parish of St. Mary's.

When I was growing up in the 1940s and early '50s the rivalry between the Sacred Heart Catholics (the Highholders) and the Lutherans of First English and Peace Lutheran (the Plattdeutschers) was coming to a close. But I was told that in the '30s and '40s whenever Catholics from the 6th Ward chose to enter Lutheran territory east of the Ohio Street, gang fights would usually break out.

In 1898 during the Oshkosh Woodworker's trial, Oshkosh ethnic history was again reshaped when a new and cheaper labor force - the Volga Germans - was recruited by George Paine.

Evangelical Lutherans from Hesse, part of Germany in the 18th century, responded to an invitation from Catherine the

Great of Russia to move to the Volga River area to form a frontier population barrier against the Cossacks. In return for their services, they were given religious freedom, exemption from taxation and other privileges. They soon acclimated themselves to their new environment retaining their own language and culture and prospered.

Some years later they became victims of the Czar Alexander's Reunification Program under which they were ordered to adopt the Russian language and the Russian Orthodox religion and to register for the draft.

In response, many began moving to the United States. One group of four happened to be in Oshkosh in 1898 during the strike, apparently scouting new settlement locations.

The group was brought to the attention of George Paine, and when they met, he encouraged the newcomers to return to Russia and recruit a body of their fellow villagers to move to Oshkosh as replacement workers at the Paine Lumber Company.

They returned to Russia, organized a party and the group immigrated to Oshkosh. The company provided the first immigrant workers with housing and encouraged them to send for others. Most of the new workers went to work for Paine and eventually occupied a neighborhood across the river from the factory south of the Algoma Street Bridge.

Sawyer Street was the main thorough way of their neighborhood which stretched south and west to the city limits and came to be known as Little Russia.

The Germans from Russia eventually built an Evangelical church, Zion Lutheran, and transplanted many of their customs from their adopted Russian homeland to their new home in Oshkosh.

The unionized Bohemians on the south side felt intense hostility against the west side scabs from Russia and an

Oshkosh ethnic conflict flared anew. One Highholder remarked that the Rooshians were perceived in this community as peasants and barbarians and he and his friends had nothing to do with them. The Volga Germans responded with negative feelings of their own about the bohunks of the 6th Ward and those bitter divisions continued well into the 20th century.

A historical marker in Rochlin Park dedicated in 1991 memorializes the Volga Germans who became known as the west siders.

Former Attorney General for the state of Wisconsin, Peg Lautenschlager, who comes from a west side Volga German family, chronicled the history of the group and their assimilation into American culture in a thesis she wrote while a student at Lake Forest College in Illinois.

Between 1899 and 1914 Oshkosh's west side developed very distinct boundaries: to the east it was bound by the Fox River; to the north, by West Algoma Street; and the south by First Avenue.

The West Side Volga Germans not only lived in a close community, they also worked together. The 1900 Oshkosh City Directory shows that 43.5 percent of Germans from Russia were employed by the Paine Lumber Company. By 1910 that number had risen to 81 percent. They were completely unaware that they were filling vacant positions of black-listed strikers.

Henry Ruehl was one of the young men who came to Oshkosh from the Volga. He worked for the Paine Company for 25 years.

"They had a bank where I put my money, but I lost it - $6,000 – when the bank went bust in 1929. It was the Paine Company bank. A lot of times I didn't take lunch. I thought I could work without eating. Sometimes on the way home I'd stop at Happy Johns, a tavern on Sawyer Avenue and West Algoma. For 5 cents you could get a pail of beer that filled four glasses. I always bought Oshkosh beer there to take home. We liked it the best."

Several years ago George Scheuermann, whose family moved to Oshkosh from the Volga area in Russia, visited the Soviet Union. His travel was restricted, but wherever he went, he inquired about the Volga Germans who remained in Russia. The answer was always the same. "We don't know anything about it."

The Reverend Weng, pastor of Christ Lutheran Church during the major years of immigration, would go down to the train station and meet all the newcomers who came to Oshkosh. He spoke German to them and made them feel welcome. Eventually Weng helped the West Side Volga German community establish their own church, the Zion Lutheran Church, which the congregation built on Sawyer Avenue. The traditional religious practices of the old country prevailed. All church services were conducted in German, with the men sitting on the left side, the women on the right and elders in front.

"All of that changed in the early '60s. But it was hard for the older members to give up that German service. I remember one woman protested saying, 'They don't speak English in heaven!'"

A few years after Oshkosh was incorporated in 1853, the city's German community that emigrated from Bavaria and Bohemia and Pomerania built a large building called Turner Hall.

Even today it is not uncommon to hear some of the older people speak of Armory B and the Turner Hall. Most of us have no idea of what it meant to be a "Turner." Few know that at one time the "Turners" were an important force in the city.

The name "Turner" is derived from the German "Turnverein" which was at first an athletic and social organization in Germany in the mid-19th century to help counter the oppression against working Germans that turned into the historic famous 1848 Revolution. The revolution was unsuccessful in removing the authoritarian Royal Monarchies in not only Germany but throughout most of Europe resulting in mass migration to our country.

When it was brought to America in the middle part of the 19th century the Turnverein flourished in Milwaukee and the eastern part of the state and was organized in Oshkosh in the late 1860s.

The iconic symbol of the Turnverein was its creation of Turner Halls that were sprinkled throughout Wisconsin and a handful of other states. The halls served as gymnasiums, lecture centers, theaters, music halls and a source of political mobilization. In the late 19th century the Turners played a role in American public education and in the labor movement. Later the Halls would figure prominently in the ranks of both the progressive and socialist movements of the early 20th century.

Turner Halls could be found in every large German-American community in the 19th century. Under the motto's sound mind in a sound body, they also served as social and intellectual meeting places. Oshkosh had not one, but two Turner Halls, one on the north side of the city on the corner of Merritt and Jefferson, the other on the south side on the southeast corner of 10th and South Main.

The first of the Turner Halls was built in 1874 in the downtown section of Oshkosh. It was a wooden structure and it lasted until 1883 when it was turned into an opera house that proved less than successful. Seven years later in 1890 the Turner Society turned to William Waters to design an imposing brick structure on the old site on the corner of Merritt and Jefferson streets.

Much larger than the 1874 structure the new hall was capable of providing the full range of Turner activities much like the hall in downtown Milwaukee.

North side Turner Hall

With the advent of World War I, the Turner societies were not able to survive the anti-German movement, not only in Oshkosh but throughout the country. That overshadowed the physical and intellectual objectives of the founding members, and the members decided to sell it to the National Guard in 1901. It was used as Armory B until it was sold to Montgomery Ward in 1961. A new National Guard Armory was built that year and is located on Osborn Street where it still is in operation.

In 1894 Waters also drafted plans for another hall on the south side of town. It was located on the southeast corner of 10th and South Main.

South side Turner Hall

It was an immense and grandiose wooden structure in the then popular Queen Anne style, sporting a soaring corner tower. It was sold to the Godshall Paper Company again because of the anti-German feelings due to the conflict in World War I. Regrettably, a fire destroyed the building in January of 1920. It was considered one of the most admired and well-known buildings in the city.

Chapter Four
Women's Suffrage

The women's suffrage movement was a decades-long fight to win the vote for women. It took activists and reformers on the state and local level nearly one hundred years to win that right, and the campaign was not easy. Disagreements over strategy threatened to cripple the movement more than once.

The movement began in earnest in the decades before the Civil War when most states had extended the franchise to all white men regardless of how much money or property they had. The arrangement did not include women because the prevailing view of the time was that a "true" woman was a pious and submissive wife and mother concerned exclusively with home and family.

Oshkosh's Jessie Jack Hooper was an important force in this movement along with others who helped bring about the passage of the 19th Amendment that gave women the right to vote.

Jessie Jack Hooper was an Iowa transplant who eventually married Ben Hooper of Oshkosh after visiting our city with her sister. Soon after, she got involved in women's clubs which were prominent in small cities like Oshkosh.

She became a member of numerous clubs that advocating for better schools, public health programs and other community affairs that would help those in need. She signed petitions, buttonholed city alderman and ward commissioners but it didn't take long for her to realize that men in charge of city government had little interest in what she or other women wanted.

Like others, Jessie soon got tired of going on pilgrimages when they rarely got what they asked for. But through these efforts she began to see how women could still make a difference.

She said she observed that men in politics were mostly concerned with policies that involved money. Women were more interested how government could improve people's lives.

Jessie Jack Hooper

She soon begin lobbying state legislators for women's suffrage, making speeches throughout the state and doing everything she could to work up sentiment for suffrage. She campaigned throughout the state, wrote letters to state legislators in hopes of earning the right to vote for women.

Mrs. Hooper continued as the principal suffrage speaker of

the state and in 1915 was invited and attended the Annual Suffrage Convention in Washington D.C.

The following summer Jessie invited a group of area suffragists to make a trip up the Wolf River in her husband's boat. It was decorated with pennants and suffrage banners hoping to attract attention along the way. They passed out literature, made converts and enjoyed meeting people.

In 1917, during World War I, Jessie chaired the Oshkosh Women's Patriotic League. She rolled bandages for the Red Cross, spoke all over Wisconsin for food conservation (meatless Mondays and Wheatless Wednesdays that were authorized during parts of WWI) and urging suffragists to ask those running for public office where they stood on Women's Suffrage.

Carrie Chapman Catt, president of the National Women's Suffrage Association, formerly of Ripon, appointed Mrs. Hooper and Minnie Fisher Cunningham, two nationally recognized suffragists to tour Arizona, Nevada, New Mexico and Utah to persuade their governors to call a special session of the state legislature to ratify the proposed 19th Amendment hoping to get the required 36 states for ratification.

A year later in 1920 the 19th Amendment was finally ratified when Tennessee became the 36th state to pass the Amendment as required by the U.S. Constitution granting women the right to vote.

The Oshkosh League of Women Voters was one of the earliest leagues organized in Wisconsin. The League encouraged women to use their voting privileges and were encouraged to attend citizenship classes to better understand their rights under the new law.

By 1927, the organization had 500 members and was campaigning for the classification and the purification of milk and better garbage collection and disposal. It also sponsored lectures on municipal government and advocated city zoning laws and the use of the voting machine.

In more recent years, the League has arranged candidate meetings and worked for an efficient city government, supporting city planning including street renaming and renumbering.

In 1922 Hooper was selected by the Democratic Party of Wisconsin to run as their candidate for U.S. Senator against the popular Robert LaFollette even though she had never been a member of a political party.

Although she was a leader of a nonpartisan group, she accepted knowing she would be a "sacrificial lamb." No man wanted to run against LaFollette but Jessie felt a women's voice needed to be heard.

Despite losing by a landslide, Jessie was proud to have blazed a trail that she hoped other women would follow.

There were others from Oshkosh whose efforts resulted in Wisconsin being the first state to ratify the proposed 19th Amendment. Among those was Sophie Gudden, an immigrant from Germany.

Sophie Gudden arrived in Oshkosh in the 1880s as a medical doctor, and she and her husband, also a doctor of medicine, set up their practice in the town of Black Wolf south of the city, but eventually moved their practice in Oshkosh. She soon became a member of the exclusive Twentieth Century Club, an exclusive women's club in the city, limited to those whose education and standing in the community was considered suitable.

Sophie, as one of the leading members of the club, soon became an advocate for better schools and public health programs. She signed petitions, talked to aldermen and ward commissioners but, like many other women of the time, found the men in charge of city government, while always polite, had little interest in what the women's group wanted because they had no vote.

She soon got tired of joining others in their attempts to convince state legislators and decided, mostly on her own, to concentrate her efforts on securing the vote for women. She, like Jessie Jack Hooper, became a suffrage activist and remained so until the 19th Amendment was passed.

Sophie also became active to help state-wide workers securing their rights through the Wisconsin Consumer League. An 8 hour day, a minimum wage for women and improved child labor laws were among her concerns.

Like so many activists, she realized that their voice would not be heard unless women possessed the most fundamental right of citizenship.

She was soon joined by Jessie Jack Hooper, the most prominent of the suffragists, although Gudden would later be recognized as the quiet hero by those involved in the suffrage campaign in Wisconsin.

There were others in Oshkosh besides Hooper and Gudden who worked to convert men towards women suffrage. Sarah James and her sisters, Harriet and Clara, as well as Rose Swart, an esteemed teacher and administrator at the Oshkosh Normal School, were active as well.

Suffrage activism in Oshkosh was picked up by the *Milwaukee Journal* in the summer of 1917.

"With a few months, the Oshkosh Equal Suffrage League has grown from a membership of sixty interested women to over two hundred who are clamoring for the right at the polls after Sarah James, Sophie Gudden and Rose Swart had addressed a suffrage meeting at the Pabst Theater in Milwaukee."

"In Oshkosh," according the Milwaukee paper, "league

members built a float for the 4th of July parade, assembled an exhibit at the county fair, brought nationally-known women's rights speakers such as Jenkins Lloyd Jones and British suffrage activist, Sylvia Pankhurst to Oshkosh. They hit the campaign trails in Winnebago County on land via a specially decorated automobile, and in water via a steam launch."

When the European War began in 1914, Gudden worried about her German relatives, and the prolonging of the war soon aggravated her health. No longer mobile and unable to attend meetings, Gudden sent suffrage materials to Wisconsin's English and German newspapers. In 1916 she focused only on the German press.

In Sophia Gudden's last year, she was confined to a wheel chair due to arterial sclerosis. By the time the Wisconsin Legislature ratified women's suffrage on June of 1919, Gudden was too ill to celebrate. She died July 23 of that year, more than 100 years ago.

The Women's Movement did not stop with the 19th Amendment. The decades that followed saw women demonstrating for equal job opportunities, equal pay and advancement, child care services and access to contraception. The new birth control pill freed many women from unwanted pregnancies and gave them many more choices and freedom in their personal life and impacted the women's role in the family.

Since many of these accomplishments and changes took effect and have been largely accepted in our society, many women today have a difficult time believing that life was much different for their grandmothers and those who came before.

Chapter Five
Racial Segregation

Oshkosh was a "sundown town" in the 1940s and '50s where African-Americans were not welcome to stay overnight. Those who challenged this custom put themselves at grave risk. Although African-American fishermen who drove to Oshkosh from Milwaukee and the Racine areas to cast their lines in the Fox River were tolerated during the day but knew they were not welcomed after sunset.

Uncomfortable as it is to admit for those of us who lived here at the time, racial prejudice simmered here throughout the '40s and '50s and into the 1960s. Some, if not much of this was due to the television coverage of riots in Watts, Detroit, Newark and in the neighboring city of Milwaukee during the 1960s. As a result fear of African Americans intensified.

To help us understand the history of racial segregation in our city we need to go back to the 1920s when the Ku Klux Klan played an important role in the history of Oshkosh.

Yes, the white robed and hooded Ku Klux Klan.

The Klan was founded the shortly after the Civil War by Confederate veterans in response to the passage of the 14th and 15th Amendments that granted equal protection of the law and voting rights for former enslaved people. But that didn't stop the Klan from restoring white supremacy in many of these former Confederate states. Violence was often used to intimidate the formerly enslaved black Americans. Lynchings were common.

Dressed up in white robes and sheets designed to frighten blacks and to prevent identification by the occupying federal troops in former Confederate states, Klansmen whipped and killed freedmen and their white supporters in nighttime raids in the South.

Realizing something had to be done, Congress, in 1871, passed a law authorizing President Ulysses S. Grant to use military force to suppress the KKK resulting in thousands of arrests and lessening the effectiveness of the organization.

Fifty years later, a resurgence of Klan activity occurred in the northern part of the country including cities like Oshkosh.

With the influx of new immigrant groups from southern and eastern Europe, along with Catholics, Jews, African Americans and organized labor, the Klan began burning crosses, staging rallies, organizing parades and marches denouncing them as enemies of the American Republic. There was also a fear of communism inspired by the Bolshevik recent triumph in Russia in 1917.

When the second Klan peaked in the 1920s its membership exceeded four million and profits rolled in from the sale of the memberships, regalia, costumes, publications and rituals.

By the year 1924, membership in the Klan in Oshkosh reached over 4,000 residents, approximately one out of every seven people living here. Cross burning occurred often in the city during the mid-1920s. It was used by the Klan to attract attention and arouse interest in the organization. The Klan had three offices in the city to enlist membership. One was on West Algoma (Oshkosh Avenue) the other two were on the north and south sides of town.

The Klan drew members by upholding their idea of Christian morality. Their hatred of blacks, Catholics, Jews and foreigners and other non-Protestant groups was central in their beliefs. And they also asked all Americans to uphold the laws of this country including the recent passage of the 18th Amendment prohibiting the drinking and sale of alcoholic beverages.

The message worked in many communities in the north including here in Oshkosh.

Initiation of new members was also held outside of town to attract area residents as well. In July of 1924, large cross burnings occurred on the Lange farm south of the city and in a field of another farm along Junction A on the way to Neenah. These outings attracted the attention of those driving in the area, and cars would usually stop to see what was going on, frequently resulting in increased Klan memberships.

Oshkosh was the center of Klan activity in the state and was chosen by the KKK to have their state meeting here.

According the *Oshkosh Northwestern* of February 26, 1925, "Between 300 and 500 Knights of the Ku Klux Klan will meet in Oshkosh for a two-day conference Saturday and Sunday. The meeting is being held for the purpose of outlining a spring expansion campaign."

"On July 4, 1925 a huge gathering is being arranged by the Klan and multiple celebrations are planned," according to the same newspaper. "Nationally known men, including Senator Mayfield of Texas, ex-Governor Walker of Georgia, and Judge Orison of Indianapolis will be the speakers at the rally at the fairgrounds here. Large delegations will be present from Illinois, Ohio, Indiana, Kentucky, Kansas, Minnesota, Iowa, Michigan, and North and South Dakota along with thousand in attendance from Wisconsin. It is expected that a crowd of 135,000 people will be here for the event."

Ku Klux Klan at the County Fairgrounds in Oshkosh

"There will also be a parade. The organizer said that it will be eight miles long. Thousands will take part and all will be robed in the Ku Klux Klan regalia. The women will parade separately and also be in a hooded uniform."

My dad, fascinated with the stories he read and heard, watched the entire parade on High Street. He was 17 at the time.

Harry P. Hurst, author of the booklet, Random Thoughts of Nordheim stated that: "Back in 1926 the Oshkosh Klavern of the Ku Klux Klan held a state conclave right on Jackson Drive. It was on the Stilson farm, a half-mile north of the city limits on the west side of the road. That was Just across the road from Nordheim. The fields were one mass of tents – between 10,000 and 15,000 people showed up for the meeting. Truckloads of straw were brought in and a large cross was planted on the top of it and set on fire."

"Although the black population of Wisconsin numbered only 5,000, the Klan took advantage of any prejudices that presented themselves. It also was hostile to the Catholic Church, Jews and foreigners."

"I lived on the south side of Oshkosh in the Sixth Ward (also known as The Bloody Sixth). I remember seeing them riding around in cars which was a luxury in those days. Our neighborhood was predominantly Catholic and our parents warned us all to stay in our yards and not go near them if they came around. I heard of a few crosses being burned, but I never saw one for myself. It was claimed that the Klan rescued young Catholic girls from going to the convent to become nuns."

An event that many of us do remember also helps to tell the story of race relations in our city. It was a dramatic civil rights demonstration that took place in 1968 at UW-O, at that time known as the Wisconsin State University at Oshkosh.

Ninety-four African-American students staged a sit-in protest in the university's president's office demanding action on racial discrimination on campus. The protest shocked the predominately white Oshkosh community and came to be known as "Black Thursday."

Citizens of Oshkosh and surrounding communities, most of whom had only previously witnessed the civil rights movement of the 1960s through news broadcasts carried through their television sets, were stunned by the demonstration and the resulting damage.

The young black students who enrolled at UW-Oshkosh in record numbers in the fall of 1968 knew little of the racial tensions that gripped the city and most of Northeast Wisconsin prior to their arrival. As the number of black students grew, so did instances of unfavorable treatment from professors and coaches and from the harassment on campus from fellow students. And the residents of Oshkosh continued to practice a northern version of Jim Crow, denying their new black neighbors housing, entertainment, employment and basic services.

Hostilities from students and townspeople, while mostly subdued when the numbers of African-American students on campus was small, the number increased markedly in the fall of 1968. Black students who returned to Oshkosh in the fall semester could not help notice a new uneasiness on the campus and in the community.

With the addition of nearly fifty new black freshmen, the African-American presence was now inescapable. Racial tensions inevitably intensified. The word "nigger" was regularly used on campus, and when they ventured outside the university grounds a conflict was bound to happen.

It all came to a head in the fall semester of 1968. The college president, Roger Guiles, responded to the occupation of his office by expelling all 94 students, banning all 94 from the campus.

Black Thursday, as it was called, and its aftershock dealt a serious blow to the university and had a detrimental effect on Oshkosh's reputation.

To be clear, racial tensions did not always exist in Oshkosh. The Shadds, a black family, who once lived here is a story worth telling.

I often heard stories of the Shadds and of their son who was touted as one of the best high school basketball players ever to play for Oshkosh High.

I often brought it up to others who I thought may have lived during the time, but everyone I asked had no idea who they were, that is, until a fellow golfer and I were in the same foursome in a league at the Utica Golf Course.

This story is from a conversation I had with Dale Wood a week or so later. When I asked if he ever heard of the Shadd family, he said that he played basketball with their son Bill.

As Dale tells his story we must remember there were few

blacks living in Oshkosh at the time, perhaps only the Shadd family. As a result blacks did not pose a threat to our community as many apparently did in the late 1960s.

This is Dale Wood's story.

The Shadd family moved to Oshkosh sometime in the 1920s and lived on King Street. They were, to the best of my knowledge, the first Negro family to do so. The father went to work shining shoes and keeping the floor clean at the Modern Barbershop on Washington Boulevard across the street from the Eagle's Club. The mother kept house and was getting their son Bill ready to enter Merrill School.

When Bill was in grade school, he caught the attention of Jack Nussbaum, the varsity basketball coach at Oshkosh High. Coach Nussbaum, always on the lookout for players who could help his team, came to watch young Bill play and liked what he saw. He knew Bill would become an outstanding high school basketball player if he continued to work on his game. There was one other thing Coach Nussbaum noticed about this precocious lad that concerned him; Bill was awfully thin.

He decided to visit the Shadd family and after introductions and some talk about basketball, he asked if it would be all right if their son came to his house for the evening meal. The parents gave their consent. By the time Bill entered high school he was filled out and in good physical shape.

Bill played both forward and guard on the high school team and was an outstanding ballplayer at either of these positions. When he came off the floor for a short rest, he always received a standing ovation, home or away. He was that good.

The high school played in the old high school gym during my freshmen year. The gym, with its running track circling the gym on the second floor, was located in the Red Brick building that was attached to what is the present City Hall. In 1937, the high school started to play its games in the Recreation Gym that faces Division Street.

We had a good team during those years. In addition to Shadd and myself, others who played regularly were Eddie Erban who played professional basketball for a team in Toledo and later with the Oshkosh All Stars. Bob Roth brought up the ball and was our main guard during those years. Bob was a member of the University of Wisconsin basketball team that won the NCAA Basketball Championship in 1941 by defeating a favorite Washington State team. Featured on that Wisconsin team were Gene Englund, who later played professionally with the Oshkosh All Stars and the Boston Celtics, and Johnny Kotz, a first team All-Conference player at the university, who also played professionally. After serving in World War II, Bob Roth, along with another local favorite, Len Heinbigner, played for the Oshkosh Giants in the Wisconsin State League.

The Nussbaums had 20 of us over for dinner during Bill's senior year in 1939 after the team won the Conference Championship. To celebrate, Shadd was voted captain for the year. He was also an all-conference player each of the three years he played for Oshkosh High.

After completing his high school degree, Bill had a basketball scholarship offer to attend a college in Florida. The next time we ran into each other was at his mother's funeral. We talked about the good old days and he wanted to know how everyone was doing. I'll never forget his parting words. "I never knew how good I had it here." Although he didn't say, it was more than likely due to the type of treatment he and others of his race received in a segregated Jim Crow south.

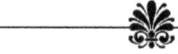

Chapter Six
Prohibition

The 18th Amendment passed on January 16, 1919 prohibited the production, importation, transportation, and sale of alcoholic beverages in the United States. Congress then passed the Volstead Act to enforce the amendment.

Most of the organized efforts supporting Prohibition involved religious groups who desired to heal what they saw as an ill society beset by alcoholic related problems such as alcoholism, health, family violence, criminality and public morals.

Opposition was from the beer industry and from German Catholic and Lutheran communities. The influence in preventing the "dryness of American" diminished in 1917 following the entry of the U.S. into the First World War against Germany.

But soon after the war was over and the Amendment passed, the illegal manufacturing and sale of liquor known as bootlegging went on throughout the decade of the 1920s along with the operation of speakeasies selling illegal alcohol.

Prohibition proved difficult to enforce and failed to have the intended effect of eliminating crime and other societal problems. To the contrary it led to a rise in organized crime as the bootlegging of alcohol became a lucrative business.

The most notorious example of this was the Chicago gangster Al Capone who earned a staggering $60 million annually from bootleg operations and speakeasies.

Fourteen years later on December 5, 1933 the 21st Amendment ended Prohibition, though it continued in some states. This was the only time in American history in which a constitutional amendment was passed for the purpose repealing another.

Clarence Jungwirth, an Oshkosh historian, along with others, describe the reactions of many in Oshkosh after the passage of this new law.

"Inky" as he was known, was born in 1919 and grew up during the years of Prohibition and lived a few blocks east of the Sacred Heart Church, the center of the 6th Ward. His research and his own experiences help us understand this period almost forgotten in our city's history.

"Many of the people who came to Oshkosh were from Europe. They came from a drinking culture. Beer was deeply ingrained in the European culture. And that meant they didn't need to rely on the corner saloon to keep them in beer. They knew how to brew their own."

"My grandparents made their own beer. This was common in the district. The 6th Ward neighborhood was the biggest producer of booze, bathtub gin and beer in the city. It was all homemade of course."

"My grandpa had a basement and he'd ferment his beer in big crock jars. He had crocks upon crocks of beer in his house. They even had their own bottling process."

"In 1919 there were 134 taverns in Oshkosh. They were then called Sample Rooms. They did not close during the Prohibition years. They simply changed to Soda Emporiums. Pop was sold on top of the bar and beer was sold beneath the bar. You could drink beer at the bar if the owner knew you."

"Cops in Oshkosh never raided the taverns unless the federal revenue agents came to town and made them do it. At this time cops walked the beat and knew what was going on in the neighborhood. When possible, cops were assigned a beat in their own neighborhood. Chief of Police, Bill Golz, who grew up on the south side allowed this to happen."

"The making of moonshine (illegally distilled corn whiskey) was a prosperous business enterprise in the ward during those years. It was an easy way to make a dollar or two. Wages in the lumber mills were low especially after the

Depression set in. Any extra income would help keep body and soul together."

"It is estimated by some of the 'old timers' in the ward that 50 percent of the families were involved in making the moonshine for home consumption or for sale in taverns or with neighbors and friends. Mostly women were involved as the men had to work long hours in the mills."

"There were many raids on the private homes by Prohibition agents in an attempt to stamp out the moonshine-making business. An alarm system was developed in the ward. When a home was being raided the word was spread by word-of-mouth and by telephones throughout the neighborhoods. The people who had moonshine in their homes would conceal it or get rid of it."

"Crime, other than for those who dabbled in the illegal liquor business, was almost non-existent in the 6th Ward. If you did commit a crime you had to go to confession. To receive absolution you would have to repay any damage incurred by your crime. Beat cops were powerful forces in Catholic neighborhoods as were families and neighbors. So this kind of discipline was inherent in the culture of the ward."

Harry Hurst, the author of *Random Thoughts of Nordheim* wrote that he also had first-hand information on prohibition in Oshkosh.

"In the late 1920s we were about to lose our house on the south side. My mother decided to go into the moonshine business. We bought our booze from an old German guy on 8th Street for five dollars a gallon and sold it for one dollar a pint. She could make three dollars on a gallon which was good money if you could get everyone to pay. Of course, you always had problems with the 'deadbeats' who wouldn't pay. If they didn't pay you had no recourse because you were in an illegal business. If you tried to pressure the deadbeats, they could turn you in. Fortunately, we did make enough money to live."

"One day a nice old guy who was a regular paid with a check which was very rare in those days. My mother didn't want to take it but there wasn't much choice – you were caught between a rock and a hard place. After he left, she sent my sister to the store for food with the check. Before she left she checked the mailbox on her way out. There was a note in the box which read: 'Dear Mrs. Hurst, if you try to cash this check, I have evidence against you, signed Mr. C. We never saw the guy again."

"Many times when I was seven or eight years old, I would pick up moonshine in my coaster wagon. All the bootleggers had ways of hiding their stuff. The old German we bought from had two walls in his cellar lined with rabbit cages. One section was hinged so it would swing out and expose a small room where he kept his stuff. At our house we had steps going upstairs with a three-by-three landing about a foot high. Two of the tongue and groove boards would slide out. We kept our booze in there. The old German we bought from was one of only a few people in the Sixth Ward to have a new car in those days."

When The 18th Amendment was passed in 1920, the cops in Oshkosh showed little interest in Prohibition violations. Even the mayor was against the new law. He did, after all, hoped to be reelected. The feds, whose responsibility was to enforce this dry law, didn't trust them.

By 1921 the city's scandalous reputation as a place where Prohibition did not apply brought in federal agents to enforce the law of the land.

So on the night of August 26, 1921, as reported by *Oshkosh Beer Timeline,* who has published stories of the history of beer, breweries and saloons in Oshkosh, the federal agents made their first major raids in Oshkosh. They aimed their initial thrusts at the most prominent targets including the Annex Thirst Parlor (now Oblio's Lounge) on the north side and Witzkes on the south side.

That night they weren't drinking soda at the Annex Thirst Parlor, they were having their usual rounds of whiskey. When the agents rushed in the owner didn't even try to hide it. They arrested him and then traveled a few blocks south on Main Street where they arrested Fred Rahr. His saloon was owned by the Rahr Brewing Company.

The agents quickly spread across town going after bars either owned by or connected to a brewery. Word traveled fast and many of the speakeasies decided to shut their doors.

They raided about a dozen suspected speakeasies that night but most were closed. The agents didn't understand why they closed as early as 9 at night including one of their main targets, Witzkes.

The following morning the agents delivered their liquid evidence to City Hall for safe keeping where they were met by the city's mayor. He wasn't happy and lit into the agents. He stated Oshkosh was not sympathetic with Prohibition enforcement.

Welcome to Oshkosh.

Although it was impossible to ignore the dry law, that didn't stop the residents of Oshkosh from trying. When Prohibition began in 1920, there were close to 100 licensed saloons in the city. A year later, nearly all of them were still in operation. They were now licensed as soft drink parlors. The distinction meant nothing.

An Oshkosh bootlegger interviewed in 1980 put it this way when asked to answer this question: How many saloons sold alcohol illegally in Oshkosh during Prohibition?

"Only about a hundred percent."

The disregard for the new law hadn't gone unnoticed by federal agents, neither had the complacency of local law enforcement. Police in Oshkosh had a habit of looking the other way when it came to illegal liquor. Their leniency didn't sit well with the feds.

When the raids continued the following day, it involved a saloon operated by Joseph Riedy at 1226 Oshkosh Avenue. When they broke in, a woman grabbed a bottle off the back bar and bolted to the apartment upstairs. The bar still stands. It's now Gorilla's Bar. And the same back bar where the woman grabbed the bottle of Sunny Brook; both the bottle and the back bar are still there.

They then raided the old Hartske saloon before it was named My Brother's Place on High and Osceola where the Blackhawk Commons now stands. A block west of Hartske's, they invaded the Giant Grip Saloon on High Avenue. They discovered four pints of moonshine hidden under the bar and a pint of legal liquor issued to the owner on a doctor's prescription. Getting booze on prescription was fairly common in Wisconsin during Prohibition. In 1922 alone, Wisconsin druggists doted out 75,000 gallons of whiskey. It was the medical marijuana of its day.

Whether or not the feds realized it, there was a common thread linking Riedy's Bar and the saloon operated by Edward Hartske. The common thread was both places were owned by the Rahr Brewing Company of Oshkosh.

Though the Rahr family steadfastly denied it, there had been much speculation in Oshkosh that their brewery was involved with bootleggers. Perhaps, the feds were sending Rahrs a message by taking out two of their "soda parlor" speakeasies.

The temperance movement was organized years before the

passage of the 18th Amendment for the purpose of curbing the consumption and the use of intoxicating liquors. Carry Nation, an icon of the movement, was one of its leading advocates.

Born in 1846, Nation was a strong 6 foot tall woman, often unhinged. When she turned violent she grew famous. Her act was to smash saloons. It began in 1900 in Kiowa, Kansas. She said God told her to go there and throw bricks at taverns. So she did.

She continued her attacks in other saloons in Kansas and received some favorable press. She refined her game by using a hatchet instead of the brick throwing. Her tool of choice came to symbolize her one-woman war against saloons and alcohol.

In 1901, Carry Nation was known nationwide. She took her act on the road. It was inevitable she would hit Oshkosh. It was said Oshkosh was the wickedest city in the state of Wisconsin if not the entire Northwest.

In 1901, she met James G. Clark, vice president of what was later known as Oshkosh B'Gosh. Clark was visiting Kansas at the time Nation was being held in a Topeka jail for running amok in saloons there. Clark went to see her. He scheduled events on July 19 and 20 for her to speak at two events owned by the Traction Company of Oshkosh. One of those events was at the Electric Park, later known to most in the city as EWECO Park. She would give her spiel, meet the locals, and make some cash selling her trinket hatchets.

As the date approached, anticipation grew. "The saloon smasher of Kansas is coming to Oshkosh," the *Daily Northwestern* stated. "This may cause some odd-127 saloon proprietors of this city to lock up their places and take to the tall timber."

Carrie Nation was on her way.

She limbered up for Oshkosh by throwing a tantrum in Fond

du Lac. There, she said Wisconsin is drowning in beer. "Every German in Wisconsin should be blown up with dynamite," she raged.

Nation marched down Fond du Lac's Main Street hissing at saloon men and their patrons. At the E.J. Schmidt saloon, she produced a hatchet and smashed a bottle of whiskey. It was all show. Schmidt grabbed her axe and threw her out. Next morning she headed north by rail.

Carrie Nation

She checked into the Athearn Hotel on the morning of July 19, 1902. She was preparing to nap when a reporter from the *Northwestern* came knocking. When interviewed she said: "You have a very beautiful city here I understand, though it is a very bad and wicked city."

It rained all the following morning. The weather kept Nation confined to her room. By noon, she decided to make her mark. In the Athearn dining room she went ballistic when a waiter handed her a menu that included a wine list. She then barked at a group of men drinking beer at a nearby table. Finally, someone found a menu without a wine list on it.

After eating, she spewed more insult. Nation railed at a young lady working the Athearn's cigar case. She said it was "a shame that a handsome girl would hand out cigars to vile smokers." She accused the girl of "helping to wreck the lives of the men."

She abused a bartender then turned to a clerk demanding to know if he was a Christian. The clerk wasn't intimidated. He smiled at her and said he thought he was. Nation stormed out.

It kept raining. Her first public appearance was scheduled in late afternoon at what was then called the Sub-Station Park, north of town. But the weather was too harsh for it. The event was hastily relocated to Armory B Hall (formerly Turner Hall) at the northeast corner of Merritt and Jefferson Streets.

After being introduced by Rev. Edward Smith of the First Congregational Church, Nation started by saying "These brewers are nearly all Germans." They come over here and are drugging the American people. Tonight this city is a place of crime, of murder. Even your hotels trap men and murder them with the drink they furnish."

She pulled out the Athearn menu that had set her off earlier in the day. She recited its wine list and the names of the different beers offered.

It was a floundering mess of a speech. The *Daily Northwestern* remarked: "She is not a literary woman and her lectures are more or less rambling and disjointed."

Sunday was supposed to be better. Nation was scheduled to appear at Electric Park in the afternoon and evening. Until then, she had time to kill in Oshkosh.

Around noon, her anger flared again. From the steps of the Athearn she could see Oshkosh paid no heed to Sunday closing laws. Saloons were running wide open. Nation had been threatening to go "slumming" since coming to town. It was time she hit the pavement.

From the front door of the Athearn she could see the Opera Buffet, a saloon run by William Bedward. She made a beeline across Opera House Square and barged through the doors of the saloon and threw a temperance rant. Bedward would have none of it. As patrons looked on, Bedward took Nation by the arm and led her back out the door. He told her he never allowed women in his saloon. And that she was no exception.

She continued to stroll down High Avenue. She stopped to harangue saloon keepers along the way, but each time was rebuffed. They told her to keep moving. None would let her inside. Worse yet, they seemed to view her with amusement.

She finally ran into a beer peddler. Seeing a beer delivery on the Sabbath triggered her. Nation lit into the man, telling him he was a fool. The beer man gave it right back. "Well, you are a damned fool," he shouted. "And everyone knows it."

Nation's High Avenue campaign ended near the corner of Jackson Street at the home of Reverend James O'Malley of St. Peter's Church. At the time, O'Malley was the leading light of Oshkosh's beleaguered temperance movement.

After her visit with O'Malley, Carrie Nation headed back to her room at the Athearn and it soon began to rain again.

The afternoon appearance at Electric Park was supposed to be the highlight of her Oshkosh visit. The amusement park just south of the city would be an ideal fit for her routine. "Farmers for miles around are planning to see her," the *Northwestern* reported. "The crowds that will gather to hear her lecture and get a sight of her will undoubtedly be very large."

She never made it to Electric Park. The rains proved too severe. Again she was moved to Armory B Hall. The farmers stayed home. The audience was sparse. Oshkosh had heard enough.

Newspapers across the country had followed Nation as she made her way to Oshkosh. Expectations ran high. The "wicked city" with the unruly saloons was bound to send her off the deep end. But folks in Oshkosh didn't take the bait. When they weren't laughing at her, they ignored her.

When she left town on Monday, the weather improved. The clouds followed her. Her next step was in Madison. While giving a speech there, the stage she stood on collapsed.

Carrie Nation passed away into obscurity. She died in Kansas in 1911.

Chapter Seven
Great Depression

*T*he *economic depression of the 1930s was the worst depression in our country's history. It threatened people's jobs, savings and even their homes and farms. At the depths of the depression, over one quarter of the American work force was out of work and many others could only find part time jobs and low pay. Because of President Hoover's dismal response to this economic downturn, he was defeated in 1932 by President Franklin Delano Roosevelt.*

My dad, who could only find part-time work during the early stages of the Depression, finally found full-time work in the mid-1930s with one of Roosevelt's New Deal programs, the WPA. At the time the city of Oshkosh received federal funds to overhaul the city's sewer system, and his job, along with others, was digging ditches for the construction of new sewers for the city. The pay was low – at the start he was paid $12 per week but it did help to pay the bills.

Along with Roosevelt's New Deal programs, George Oaks, a south sider and City Commissioner in Oshkosh was well aware of the animosity between the "haves" and "have-nots" in the city, or in the vernacular of the times, the north side versus the south side. As the Depression worsened, Oaks found himself in a position to do something for the have-nots. In 1931 he authored the Lakeshore Improvement Project along Miller's Bay. State law at the time required that any municipal expenditure greater than $500 had to be open to competitive bidding. Oaks was in a hurry to provide relief for workers without forcing them to wait out the bidding process. Although workers tended streets, sewer lines and parks, the project with the highest profile and greatest potential for work creation was the Oshkosh Lakeshore Improvement better known as the $495.

The Miller's Bay area in Menominee Park at the time was a fine wetland for frogs and ducks but not so fine for Sunday picnickers, lakeshore strollers or boaters. The aim of the project was to dredge and fill part of the marshland of Miller's Bay and construct a breakwater out into the lake. To Oaks, though, it was more important as a source of jobs to the city where the weekly wage for those still working had fallen to $10 a week.

This was before Roosevelt and his New Deal Depression era relief projects. Unemployment was high so he used his authority as Commissioner of Public Works to start work and make jobs. He expedited the project by paying contractors with city checks in amounts no larger than $495 until the contractor's fee was fully paid. It was probably the most controversial decision he or anyone else made as a local government official, and as a result made enemies, but also was widely supported by the working class.

Although he made enemies with his "slight of hand," he was elected mayor in 1933 when the city voted in the mayor-alderman form of government. He served one term and then came back to win in 1939 and served until 1946. It was his fate to lead the city in interesting times: the worst years of the Depression and the early years of World War II. "I never cared about what anyone thought of me," he said when interviewed in 1978.

The Depression years of the 1930s was also a time when men and women rode the rail looking for jobs. Many who had been forced off farms or couldn't find a job in the city would venture hundreds of miles away looking for work; sometimes on the other side of the continent. Often the only way to get there was by hopping on freight trains. Finding food was a constant problem for Hoboes, as these over-the-rail travelers were called. They often begged for food at farm houses or a house in the city. If the owner was generous the hobo would mark the lane or sidewalk if served in the city so that later hoboes would know this was a good place to be.

Never before in the history of the United States had so many of its citizens been unemployed. With no job and no home, men were forced to go where the jobs were. Hitching rides in boxcars along the nation's railways, these hobos, as they came to be known, carried their few possessions with them and lived a nomadic lifestyle. The transient nature of hobo life meant that the men were creating a new class of people. They weren't bums who refused to work or tramps who survived on hand-outs. They went to work because accepting charity would hurt their pride.

The economic instability of the 1930s meant that a factory might need a thousand workers for a short duration of time, like one month, in order to produce and fill an order, but would have to drop back to only a hundred workers after that job was complete. Factory owners relied on hobos or transient workers to fill these short-term positions. Likewise, many of the sprawling farms in the west – those unaffected by the Dust Bowl – needed to hire on additional help at planting time and harvest time. The hobos understood this and flocked to those areas in time for seasonal hiring.

Groups of hobos often set up makeshift camps near railways. Like independent communities, the hobo camps, or jungles as they were called, provided the men with a safe place to spend the night, take a bath, bandage wounds, wash out clothes, swap stories, sing songs, and share a meal. But mostly the hobo jungles offered a sense of belonging and camaraderie. Hobos could bond over their shared situation and exchange information about jobs and the locations of other hobo jungles. It was the companionship that drew the hobos together.

As the United States emerged from the Great Depression and as the country entered World War II, the nation needed every able-bodied young man it could get to help the war effort. Hobos could give up their transient lifestyle and trade their economic instability for a military career or full-time factory job. Although some hobos refused to give up their carefree lifestyle, most did, and the number of homeless unemployed men drastically decreased.

The following are stories of these over-the-rail travelers who came to Oshkosh are told by those of us who experienced their comings and goings.

This was our family's experience

Occasionally a hobo would knock at our back door to see if we could spare something to eat. We later learned they knew, through a network of exchanges and markings made and passed on by those over-the-rail travelers, the houses that would not likely turn them away.

Mother, not being a stranger to those knocks on the door, would warm up the leftovers, usually potatoes and gravy, some vegetables and sit the man down to eat. She was not always comfortable doing this but, like many others, she did it. She knew hungry, she knew poor, and she knew right from wrong.

As Ma Joad said as the Joad family moved down Route 66 in John Steinbeck's "The Grapes of Wrath" during the height of the Great Depression looking for work: "I'm learnin' one thing real good. Learnin' it all the time ever' day. If you're in trouble or hurt or in need – go to poor people. They're the only ones that'll help – the only ones."

Oshkosh had its share of these over-the-rail travelers. Some rode the Soo Line Railroad ending up in the Michigan Street area; others rode the Chicago Northwestern and temporarily settled near the mouth of the Fox River and along the shores of Lake Winnebago.

Tom Meyer, who lived on South Park Avenue near Oregon Street talks about his experiences during those growing-up days.

"Most every boy had a slingshot when I grew up. A few of us at the tender age of 9 or 10 would go down to the lake and shoot rats that we chased out of the junkyard. When we did this we were told not to go near the hobo yard located where the train tracks crossed the mouth of the Fox River.

In the late 1930s the hoboes traveled around the country looking for work and the train was their means of getting around. They would look for work or sometimes just a handout and would go to the back door of homes close to the tracks, sometimes beyond, asking for work and food. They were known to put a white chalk mark on the curb of houses where they might have gotten a good reception. After a few days they would jump back on the train and a new batch would arrive.

Clarence "Inky" Jungwirth talks about those over-the-rail travelers.

During the Great Depression of the 1930s, "riding the rail" was an expression often heard in places like Oshkosh. It referred to the methods of travel used by many of the unemployed or better known as hoboes or bums. The traveled in railroad box cars that steamed their way through Oshkosh on the Chicago Northwestern or Soo Line tracks looking for work, a meal, anything to keep the body and soul together. It was a tragic sight repeated across the entire country. They were desperate men transporting themselves from here to there.

If the box cars were locked or full of goods, these over-the-rail travelers would lie on the rods under the railroad car. These rods were used under the box car for reinforcement. It was, to say the least, a precarious perch. The men would be subject to dust, rocks and other debris as the train traveled at high speeds in the country side. They had to, with all the strength they could muster, hang on tightly. The alternative was to be maimed or killed. Desperate people often "throw the dice" and take their chances.

When the riders reached the train marshaling yards, they had to contend with the railroad detectives who would march them off to the local jail on vagrancy charges. The ones not apprehended fled to the "hobo camps" scattered at various places along the railroad tracks. It was here they rested, ate a bit of food and discussed the events of the day.

As a teenager during the Great Depression I saw those who rode the rails. They would walk the streets of Oshkosh looking for a hot meal and willing to pay for it by working around the house. I remember my mother once being approached by a hobo asking if he could do some work for a little food. My mother obliged. He was an elderly man but seemed to be a real gentleman. He did a little work for my mother who then gave him a big meal.

These hobos, these bums were not the dregs of society as many thought, but were forced by the dreary economic circumstances outside their control to live by their own wits. They developed a code on the road. It was a marking on the sidewalk in front of a house where they would, in all likelihood, receive a friendly welcome.

It was in the poorer neighborhoods of Oshkosh where they received the best welcomes. I was 89 years old and still remember that so called "bum" who received a meal at our house through the kindness of my mother. We were also poor, but this man, down on his luck, was even poorer and in greater need.

Hezzy Munsch tells the story about the Coke bottle.

In 1943 when I was 9, we moved to Oshkosh from Weyauwega. My dad got a job at Bell Machine across the bridge on Jackson Drive. The company was converted the year before into making war materials for the government. We lived on the corner of 15th and Michigan and later moving to 10th Street across from Jefferson School.

The story is about one hot summer day for three of my friends and me. We thought it would be a good idea to go for a swim in the lake. My mother did not like me going there mainly because of the hoboes that hung out in the train yard behind the Buckstaff factory on South Main. Kids loved swimming there because the water was not deep and the user-friendly sand bars some yards out made the shallow water just right for young, inexperienced kids to swim. One could walk almost a block before being in waist high water.

Because of my mother's warning, we didn't want anyone seeing us undressing as we had heard stories, so we hid in the brush along the bank. We took off our shirts and shoes, left our shorts on and proceeded to enter the water running, jumping, splashing and having a good time as only kids and the young at heart can have.

Then it happened! I stepped on something, reached down and put my hands on a broken Coke bottle. My foot felt "funny" so I got out of the water and saw blood coming from a 2 inch horseshoe-type cut on my left foot behind my big toe. I was scared, not only because of the deep cut but because of what my mother would do since she warned me to stay away from the hoboes that camped out by the lake. I grabbed my shirt, put on my shoes and ran home. I called to Mom that I cut my foot as soon as I opened the door. By this time my shoe was soaked in blood. One look from her and off to Dr. Romberg on the corner of 9th and Oregon. After he stopped the bleeding, he stitched me up and sent us home. It took a couple of weeks for the foot to heal but to this day I look at that scar and think of the hoboes and my mother's warning.

Bob Damon talks about Buckstaff's Jungle.

In walking downtown by way of South Main Street we had to pass "Buckstaff's Jungle," a wooded area along the east side of the street directly south of the Buckstaff chair and casket company. Bordering the "jungle" on the east were the tracks of the Chicago Northwestern Railroad. This was the usual jumping off place for traveling hoboes when the train slowed before crossing the Fox River Railroad Bridge. My mother told me, warned me, never to walk on the east side of the street for fear of an unscrupulous hobo leering close by. That, of course, put the fear of God in me and became the source of all kinds of stories.

In reality, these hobos were actively unemployed men looking for work and couldn't afford transportation or a suitable place to stay. The heavily wooded "jungle" provided a perfect camping place for these transients during the summer months. I don't recall ever hearing the police having problems from these over-the-rail travelers, but then again I was at a very young age.

I also decided to include a few stories of those who were desperate to find work during the depression years of the 1930s. These are stories recalled later in life by those who rode the rails.

Archie McPerran.

We left Trout, Oregon for Nebraska.

After suffering cold for hours, the train finally stopped long enough for us to move to a closed boxcar, already occupied by others. We didn't know how many were in the car until the train got underway and the men began to like cigarettes. It was eerie seeing those lights glowing in the dark, adding to our uneasy feeling about the men sitting in rows on both sides of the car. These were men we had always referred to as bums or hoboes.

The next morning the train stopped in Billings, Montana. The bums, now our fellow travelers, cautioned us about going into some cities because of the possible arrest by railroad detectives who they referred to as railroad bulls.

Violet Greig.

I was 13 from a family of 16. Being number 13, me and my 15 year-old brother went together.

I rode on a boxcar from Minot, North Dakota to Idaho in 1935.

I can remember how excited I was as we went through the Rockies and saw my first real Christmas tree growing. Then again in Spokane, Washington, when we came to the apple orchards.

I have a lot of fond memories of that trip. We went to bakeries and wrapped bread to get free rolls and bread. "Bismarcks" were so special as I had never eaten or heard of them. We asked a man if we could have some. He gave .us a box that we took back to the jungle.

I was a girl and all the bums looked out for us. I had my hair cut short to look like a boy, and I wore bib overalls.

Walter Militch.

I was 16 and remember the day mama heard a neighbor woman say there were a lot of people trying to get into the bank. Of course, the bank was closed and mama's 300 dollars in savings was gone.

Rode the rails for five years.

I can tell you about the young lady traveling in the same boxcar with a young man and she needed a pair of shoes. When we stopped in Laramie, a middle aged bum, who had overheard the conversation, brought her back a pair of shoes that fit her nicely. The next day she was traveling with the older man.

Harvest poor treatment stories. In North Dakota, five days, not paid. Fresno grapes picked at penny a box and owed 56 cents at the end of three days. A Japanese tomato grower who wouldn't let me have two tomatoes that lay on the ground. Mowing a yard as big as a football field for a sandwich. Unloaded a truck for pieces of ham thrown away.

I remember telling a young man a few years ago about the days that I went without food, about my trials during the Depression. His comment was that that was not true, something like that could not happen in this country.

I can tell you of men so distraught, rather than ask for water, they would drink water from the ground if it was available.

Chapter Eight
Aviation

Some years ago I received a telephone call from Ruth Denow soon after returning from our winter stay in Arizona. She told me that her older brother, Fred Gafner, had some interesting stories to tell about the early years of the airport and that he soon would be arriving in Oshkosh from his home in Spokane, Washington.

This is what Fred told me that day when we met at Ruth's house, with Mrs. Denow and Fred's younger brother interjecting comments of their own.

"We lived on 20th Street between Georgia and Knapp on a ten acre farm raising dairy cows and a few other farm animals when I was growing up in the 1920s and early '30s."

"I remember when the current airport was just farmland. I also remember the time when Charles Lindbergh flew over Oshkosh. While circling the city, I and a few others would run down the street in the attempt to follow his flight. During his flight over the city, it is said he dropped a bag or a pouch filled with hundreds of messages that read: 'If Oshkosh ever wants to get on the map they better get busy and get an airport.'"

"Somewhere in the museum they have that bag that Lindbergh dropped."

"Soon after, work on the airport started."

Bob Moser, who I called some weeks following the interview with the Fred Gafner, told me when he was a mere youngster playing outside near his home he heard an airplane overhead. "The plane was wobbling as it began its descent and appeared, at least from my vantage point, wanting to land somewhere to the west near 20th Street, the area that embraced nothing but farm fields."

Excited by the prospect of seeing his first airplane up close, Bob quickly jumped on his bike and raced those few blocks to where he thought the airplane had landed.

"It was a biplane that I spotted, similar to the ones I saw in books and magazines we had at home. And the farm field where the plane set down, I would soon learn, would become the Oshkosh airport."

It was Richard Lutz of the Lutz Stone Quarry Company who saw the future in aviation in the city. Together with Florian Manor, another stunt flyer, he opened the first airport in Oshkosh on west 4th Street in 1920. It would soon, for reasons unknown at least to this writer, go out of business. In 1925 Richard purchased, with help from his father, one hundred acres of farmland on 20th Street for what was to become the Oshkosh Airport Incorporated.

"Richard Lutz, anxious to practice his acrobatic maneuvers, would be up in his airplane on those clear, sunny days delighting curious spectators watching his every move," remarked Moser.

"I was always looking forward to Lutz's acrobatic flights as a youngster growing up on 19th and Doty and Oregon Streets," remarked Moser. "He was always putting on a performance doing loops and other unconventional moves stunt flyers at the time did."

Gafner continues.

"Dick and his dad, Bob, started developing the land and began building an airport hanger. They built the hanger and graded the runways by using teams of work horses used at their Knapp Street stone quarry."

"Along with managing the airport, giving flying lessons

and practicing his aerobatic maneuvers, Lutz helped bring airline and airmail service to the Fox Valley in 1928. He later sold the airport in 1940 to Winnebago County but stayed in aviation until his death in 1965."

"I think later on, the Lutz's had more work with owning two places than they were able to handle and that is probably the reason they decided to sell the airport to the county."

Steve Wittman and his Chief Oshkosh plane

"I remember when Steve Wittman became manager of the airport in 1931. I had heard about his plane building and racing as most everyone else had at the time. I remember when Wittman landed this small airplane across the street. It had this green fuselage and yellow wings. It was a pretty plane, resembling the name given it, The Pheasant. I think they still might have it displayed in one of the airport hangers."

Bob Moser.

"I remember when Wittman became manager of the airport. I heard about his plane building and racing and I followed the midget races in Cleveland each Memorial Day on the radio. My dad was a tinsmith and one Christmas he made me an airplane hangar for all my toy airplanes. I was like many other young boys at the time. We were curious and thrilled by aviation."

When Bob Moser was young he and his friends played pickup football and baseball games across the street from the airport west of Ohio Street. This was on the north side of 20th Street. It was empty lots back then he said.

"The federal government built Quonset huts on this playing field of ours during the war years to house cadets from the local college who were taking flying lessons from Wittman and Bill Brennand. They were being prepared to see action in World War II. The Quonsets were left standing until the late 1940s when additional housing was built for the returning veterans."

We often talk about Steve Wittman and Bill Brennand as if they were the only Oshkosh aviation pioneers. But there were others who have been lost in our collective memory. One who received world-wide attention in 1932 was Oshkosh native, Clyde Lee.

For years, the challenge of trans-Atlantic flight inspired many American aviators. In Wisconsin that challenge was accepted by Clyde Lee.

Speed and distance records were all the rage in the early 1930s and the press was always on the lookout for a new Lindbergh. As an Oshkosh teenager in the early 1920s, Clyde took instruction from his cousin Roy Larsen who along with his brothers operated the nearby Larson Airport.

He barnstormed with Larsen and on his own and did all of the standard tricks – wing-walking, parachute jumping, hanging ladder stunts and death defying aerobatics. Roy Larson, whose ancestors came from Norway, always wanted to be the first to fly there. When he died at an early age, Clyde Lee, his protégé, decided if the opportunity presented itself he would do it.

In the early 1930s, Lee was building a two passenger airplane to fly over the ocean. Lee got the airplane from an employer rather than being paid wages for his work as a flying instructor. He flew his 1928 Stinson to Oshkosh to modify it for the ocean trip. He knew a larger gas tank was required so he proceeded to build a large, light weight tank and had it welded to the airplane.

When a cash prize was offered to the first airplane to fly non-stop from North America to Norway, Clyde was determined to make the flight. But first he needed some backing. He initially sought financial support from Oshkosh B'Gosh. He even painted their logo on the side of his Stinson airplane, but the clothing company didn't show the interest needed for the trip ahead. So he looked elsewhere and eventually got support from a group of Vermont businessmen. He flew from Oshkosh to the east coast, repainted the plane to read Green Mountain Boys and made final preparations for his flight.

Fred Gaffner.

"Lee was operating on a shoestring and had problems raising money for the trip. His intention was to fly from Newfoundland to Norway in pursuit of a cash prize of $25,000 offered by an Oslo newspaper. The prize was to go to the first airplane to fly non-stop from North America to Norway."

"Clyde had the airplane ready to go when there was an accident with another plane at the airport. That set Lee back another month. By the time he was ready to leave, the once favorable winds were not favorable anymore. What Lee should have decided was to wait until the following year when once again there would be strong tail winds. But he decided not to wait hoping to beat others who were thinking of competing for the prize money."

"Clyde Lee ate his meals at our house while he worked on that airplane across the street. My mother charged him fifteen cents a meal. He ran up quite a bill and told my mother when he got back from the trip he would double what he owed for the meals. He was always short of money."

Lee and is co-pilot, John Bochton, took off from Harbor Grace, Newfoundland on August 24, 1932 heading east with just enough gas but with no radio or modern navigational equipment and with an airplane and engine that had seen many hours of use. Encountering storms, cold and fog over the North Atlantic, they disappeared without a trace.

Someone in England said they heard an airplane in the distance but the authorities were never sure it was them. They figured the headwinds caused the plane to run out of fuel.

Three days later on August 27, the *Associated Press* from Oslo, Norway reported: "Morning dawned without relief to the anxiety felt for the missing fliers, Clyde Lee and John Bochton."

Authorities held a fading hope the fliers might have been delayed and yet had enough fuel to land on some isolated spot.

The following story was In the August 28 edition of the *Milwaukee Journal*.

"The pilots of the airplane, Green Mountain Boy, overdue more than 40 hours on a trans-oceanic venture were feared Sunday to have been lost somewhere in the Atlantic."

"A slim hope was expressed that Clyde Lee of Oshkosh and John Bochton of Brooklyn had come down in good order and were floating on the water or that they had landed in some isolated spot in which communications are scant."

"Airport officials also suggested that the fliers might have brought their plane down near a small vessel without wireless and were unable to transmit the news of their safety."

Bob Moser told me that his family was glued to the radio for reports of the flight. "We later learned that the Green Mountain Boy was lost at sea."

There likely were many more aviation fans in Oshkosh besides the Moser's who had their ears glued to their radios that day in August. It was history in the making as it was for many of us who followed television that day in July when an American astronaut landed on the moon.

Chapter Nine
Athearn Hotel

In February of 1866 George Athearn moved to Oshkosh from Massachusetts after serving in the Civil War. After spending some time here, he decided, with the recent loss of the new Beckwith House in December of 1880 located in downtown Oshkosh, that there was a need for a first class hotel in the city.

But to build this type of hotel, Athearn needed a group of investors to help fund the project. He could not find the necessary funding at first but some years later he and others read newspaper accounts showing many business travelers were unable to find good lodging. And it was decided, as a matter of civic pride, that Oshkosh, being the second largest city in the state, should have a first class hotel.

The architect, William Waters, who drew up plans for other hotels in the city, was hired to design this new structure that would eventually occupy a city block bordered by High, Market and Division streets.

Once completed in 1891, it would become the grandest hotel in the state north of Milwaukee.

The hotel remained a fixture in the Oshkosh business district until 1964 when it was razed, making way for a new bank.

Newspaper accounts help us understand the majesty of the Athearn.

In May of 1891, the *Daily Northwestern* gave this account of the hotel.

It is a model of elegance and beauty. Upon entering the guest finds himself in an office with handsome wood trimmings that give style to the room which is not excelled in any metropolitan hotel in the country.

The bedrooms are as fine as those found in the homes of

millionaires, and the furniture in them is oak. The bridal chamber in the hotel is the most beautiful imaginable. The furniture is of light blue and there is a parlor adjoining and it is separated from the bedroom by airy curtains.

The rear of the building is occupied by a barbershop and bar room, both are furnished in oak and have silver trimmings. There is a wine room soon to be furnished and completed and a billiard room in the basement.

The entire building is lighted by gas and heated by steam. There is an elevator and a staff of forty employees to take care of the needs of the guests.

The *Oshkosh Northwestern* of June 13, 1953, during the city's centennial celebration, stated the following.

For over a year and a half the atmosphere and appearance of the Athearn Hotel has been more and more reminiscent of the "good old days" as the elegance and traditionally excellent cuisine of hotel hospitality reappears, a result of the inspiration of a group of women whose family history is a story of hotels and fine cooking.

The glamour of dining in soft candlelight and being able to choose from a list of dishes many patrons have heard mother and grandmother describe brings back memories of yesteryear to Oshkosh. Centennial dinners are now a regular feature at the Athearn.

Costumed waitresses bring to reality a scene of gracious living enjoyed by hotel patrons over 60 years ago when the Hotel Athearn was built by George Athearn in the 1890s.

The new hotel was and still is situated across from the Grand Opera House and it was host to many famous entertainers who appeared in Oshkosh as well as visitors whose only claim to fame was the size of their bank accounts.

Atherarn Hotel

Among the notables who have signed the hotel's registry book are President William Howard Taft and his son Senator Robert Taft; Presidential hopeful William Jennings Bryan; his one-time court adversary, lawyer Clarence Darrow; Scottish comedian Harry Lauder; Irish tenor Chauncey Olcott; preacher Henry Ward Beecher; ballet dancer Pavlova; actor Otis Skinner; actresses, Maude Adams, Billie Burke and May Robson; cartoonist John T. McCutcheon; U.S. Supreme Court Chief Justice Earl Warren, and captain Richard Hobson, who made "Hobson's Choice" part of the English language.

In December of 1984 the *Northwestern* wrote a story of the Hotel Athearn and the Grand Opera House as they appeared over 70 years ago. It was entitled "Reminiscences of Monument Square." This is what was written.

When the majestic Hotel Athearn fell to demolition crews 20 years ago, downtown Oshkosh lost more than a building.

Gone was the famous English Room with its massive oak beams and elaborate mirrors. Gone were the marble foyer and the basement barbershop with its silver trimmings, oak furnishings and marble floor.

Athearn's English Room

Gone was the billiard room, which according to an 1891 newspaper surpassed the billiard room in the Milwaukee Plankington House. Gone were the railed balconies.

The Athearns' continued to own the place until 1944 when they sold it to Mr. and Mrs. Thomas Kewley. In 1952 the Kewleys offered the hotel for long-term lease with options to buy to the McCaffrey sisters of Wabasha, Minnesota.

The McCaffrey family and the Athearn suited each other. The *Oshkosh Northwestern* reported that the new managers have acquired a reputation for their fine cooking.

The hotel took on a new life with extensive repairs, remodeling and renovating kitchen. Manager Jeanne McCaffrey Hall hired Chef Piotter, who had gained a reputation from his many years at the Peacock Restaurant. She asked Margaret Wahlgren, a former buyer at the Boston Store in Oshkosh, to become the public relations manager. Mrs. Wahlgren also became a bridal consultant service in the hotel.

Mrs. Hall made sure her hotel guests were not neglected. For example she wrote a letter to all her guests on June 3, 1958, and apologized. "This is probably the only time in your life you've been a guest in a hotel and not allowed in the lobby until 10 p.m. The Women's division of the Chamber of

Commerce had taken over the entire first floor for their fund raiser, called the Powder Puff Stag Party."

Mrs. Hall arranged a $1.75 buffet supper for hotel guests in a second floor room instead.

Saturday nights were a major attraction at the hotel. Piotter says, "I remember the cooks I had. Every Saturday we featured a different country's cooking. . . Greek, English, Italian. . . and the waitresses would dress in native costumes."

The dining room was closed for dinners on Sunday evenings, but the Athearn had a banquet room up a few steps from the foyer and bar where varied groups would sponsor dances and the kitchen would provide hors d'oeuvres.

During the 1950s, the Athearn twice won first place for efficient bar operation in a national contest sponsored by the *Union Server* magazine.

The 1950s were also a time of change for the Athearn and hotels like it across America. They were getting old. Open elevator shafts and stairways were frowned on by building inspectors. Travelers expected to have a private bath, which they could find at the nation's newest invention, the drive-up motel.

Auto travel was also replacing trains and busses. Cars needed to be parked, preferably right in front of the hotel. Mrs. Hall and staff decided to go after other business. They found it at the University of Wisconsin-Oshkosh, then known as Wisconsin State College. Enrollment there was growing but dormitories were almost non-existent. The Athearn annex, connected by a walkway to the main structure, opened as a dormitory for college men in 1954.

The McCaffrey family left the Athearn in 1962. For a short time, the hotel's upper floors housed the elderly as permanent residents, but maintenance costs and failure to meet housing code standards doomed the historic building.

Long-time chef, Al "Shorty" Piotter headed the Athearn kitchen in the 1950s and reminisces what it was like then.

"There's not a place around today that compares with the Athearn. It had a fireplace in the main dining room named The English Room and it was different than any other restaurant. It had atmosphere."

Many area residents regret that the elegant Athearn Hotel was demolished in 1964. Antique collector, Jerry Kowal, comments. "It upsets a lot of us that that building was torn down. That was the most beautiful piece of Victorian architecture north of Milwaukee, and it was destroyed by local ignorance."

However, the very qualities which made the hotel a showplace – oak beamed ceilings, oak floors and fireplace mantels – also made it a firetrap 73 years after it was built. When the Athearn was built in 1891, Oshkosh was a major lumber center. The hotel's frame was therefore made of wood, an abundant and cheap commodity with a brick overlay. But to meet building codes in the 1960s, the wood structure would have had to be replaced with steel.

Unfortunately, the Athearn Hotel, designed in the Romanesque style by the well-known Oshkosh architect of the time, William Waters, is just one of many jewels lost throughout the years. Examples of other structures lost to the wrecking ball include City Hall at the corner of Otter and State streets and the Turner Hall on Merritt and Jefferson. Both were demolished the same year Hotel Athearn disappeared from the city landscape.

The Revere House, one of Oshkosh's former top hotels, came down in 1983 to make room for the Oshkosh Convention and Visitors Bureau. The original, ornate Winnebago County Courthouse with its massive tower and twin wings was replaced with a newer model in 1938. The statuesque Elk's Hall on Jefferson Street was the site of many gala events between 1914 and 1976, the year it was abandoned. Arsonists got to it in 1978 the same year it was torn down.

More recent losses include the brick Morgan Company buildings at the intersection of 6th Avenue and Oregon Street, the Coles Bashford House on Oshkosh Avenue, the birthplace of the first Republican governor of Wisconsin, and the 1923-era water tower at Menominee Park are three more recent examples of losses of historic structures in Oshkosh.

"One Month Left for Oshkosh Hotel" was the headline in the *Appleton Post Crescent* on August 2, 1964.

At the end of this month another phase of Oshkosh history will pass from reality into nostalgia and memory.

For 48 permanent residents of the Hotel Athearn, that reality ended Friday, the last day for permanent and transient patrons to live there. The English Room, the dining hall, where a President, Presidential hopefuls, noted actors and others dined under oak beams and surrounded by elaborate mirrors, will be open until the end of this month. Then, it too will pass into history.

Same will be true of the cocktail lounge and the other halls where many a wedding reception, class reunion, anniversary party or political rally or convention was held. These facilities also will be in used until August 31.

The New American Bank of Oshkosh announced Saturday it had purchased the Athearn and will tear it down to make way for a new bank building. Razing is expected to start sometime next month.

The hotel's position on Monument Square and its nearness to the city's historic Grand Opera House, now the Grand Theater, made it the mecca for such notables as well as a backdrop for political rallies.

One of the last tenants of the hotel was Mrs. Dolly Athearn, who had lived there for more than a half century. She was the widow of Fred Athearn, son of builder George W. Athearn Sr.

Large bronze chandeliers that hung from the lobby's beamed ceiling lighted the way for departing guests last week. These will be used in another unit of the hotel chain. The crystal chandeliers in the French Room were acquired from an Algoma Boulevard mansion when it was razed. These too will find use elsewhere.

Despite the fact the hotel has been gone for nearly 60 years, or maybe because of it, there is still an ongoing controversy that is still not resolved, and probably will never be.

It is said that far beneath the pavement on the corner of High and Market streets in Oshkosh there may have been a dark tunnel, rich and with lore of showgirls who once sneaked from their elegant bedrooms in the Hotel Athearn unto the stage of the Grand Opera House.

This apparently is the way it unfolded.

Lillian Fraser of Oshkosh was a hostess at the Athearn for many years and took care of Dolly Athearn, widow of Fred Athearn and daughter-in-law of George, the original hotel operator.

Mrs. Athearn lived in the historic hotel for over half a century. When it was demolished, she had no place to go and no relatives who would care for her. Mrs. Fraser took her first to the Raulf Hotel and then to Evergreen Manor, where Mrs. Frazer had become the food manager.

Mrs. Frazer says, "Dolly told me the tunnel was a very hidden thing. They used to do a lot of gambling in there, and drinking during Prohibition days. Showgirls (who stayed at the hotel) could dress and get to the Opera House without going through the Athearn (lobby)."

Carl Steiger, who has been involved in Oshkosh history

since the early 1900s, discounts that story. "I knew both George and Fred Athearn, and I never heard about a tunnel." He adds with a chuckle, "I think Dolly was smoking marijuana when she told that story."

Tom McNichol has researched much of Oshkosh history and has been closely allied with the restoration of the Grand. "I was around during Prohibition. There was drinking quite openly in the Athearn bar. No need to go to a tunnel."

A man who currently works on the Grand restoration saw a brick archway on the south wall close to High Street. It had a short recessed area but was blocked beyond that. In an early morning excursion into the basement, the area was inspected by flashlight. Since he had been in the area last, however, the wall had been cemented with new material.

Bill Schultz, another worker who has been involved in Grand restoration from the beginning, said that location bore evidence that "it had been tampered with" at one time. The brick was not the same as the original wall.

"That does not prove a tunnel," countered Richard Kempinger. He is a partner in the Yarbro-Kempinger architectural firm which is in charge of the Grand restoration. Kempinger explained that many years ago, there were shops in the basement of the Grand and other buildings along Market Street. There was an outside stairway leading down to those shops, all of which had arched windows.

In 1977-78, Yarbro-Kempinger was hired to redesign Market Street from Algoma to Pearl. "The glass was still in the windows then. We blocked off those windows and that's what those workmen saw."

Robert M. Barker, president of the Valley Bank (formerly New American) which now stands where the Athearn once did, said he came to Oshkosh in 1969, five years too late to know what happened at the demolition. No one associated with the bank in 1964 has been able to tell if tunnel evidence came to light at that time.

Newspaper, library and museum archive files are all mute on the subject.

Department of Public Works engineer, Ed Potempa, checked blueprints of sewer mains placed in the area. He said in 1974 the city installed a sewer main on Market Street from Pearl to the north end of High Street. This would have covered the portion of the street under which the tunnel lay. The sewer pipe replaced one that had been laid in 1890, the year before the Athearn was built.

"We had to go down nine feet (instead of the usual six) because of other utility mains in the area," explained Potempa. He heard nothing about a tunnel at that time, although he said he would check with workers who were involved in the actual digging.

The possibility also has been discussed with Al "Shorty" Piotter, Margaret Wahlgren, Nile Johnson and Agatha Bloechl, all former employees of the Athearn. Others questioned include Ed Kienast, whose demolition company prepared the adjacent building to the Grand for restoration and Orville Bergman, lumber yard owner in Van Dyne, who supposedly had been in the tunnel in his youth. Every lead turned out to be fruitless.

But Julie Johnson in her book, "Oshkosh Down Under: Basement Businesses and the tunnel from the Hotel Athearn to the Grand Opera House" published in 2002 found other sources to suggest there was a tunnel.

She states that the tunnel from the Athearn Hotel to the Grand Opera House provided obvious benefits to the Grand performers including safety from crowds and protection from inclement weather. It also offered discreet runs to the Grand for afternoon rehearsals and performances. And for guests staying at the Athearn, this may have been a very convenient way of attending the performances across the street.

"Some believe it preposterous that there was a tunnel. But what many do not realize is that tunnels did and still exist in Oshkosh. One such tunnel was located between the old Mercy Medical Center on Hazel Street and the School of Nursing, a building since razed. The other is the much traveled tunnel between the courthouse and the safety building on Jackson."

There were a number of people interviewed for Julie's book that tend to validate the existence of the tunnel. Prominent among those was Anna "Dolly" Athearn. Dolly spoke of this tunnel to Lillian Fraser, a long-time employee and a personal friend. Marge Wahlgren, also a long-time employee at the hotel remembers Dolly telling her that the showgirls used it and they did a lot of gambling in there.

Bob Reif, nephew to Dolly, recalls that after Dolly left the hotel just before it was being torn down, we would see each other on Main Street and talk. She told me about the tunnel from the hotel to the Grand and that there were three tunnels altogether, and they had renting shops in them.

In a phone conversation Julie had with Orville Bergman, he said he recollects going to the Athearn Hotel with his father. "The next thing I knew we were in a tunnel and at the Opera House."

"Barb Marin, the granddaughter of Al Dunham, owner of the Dunham Fulton Sporting Goods Store on the corner of Ceape and Main, first talked about the railroad tunnel that was next to the store. She then went on to say that most people younger than me would not remember that tunnel and the same goes for the tunnel from down under. I remember going from the Athearn under the street to our dance recitals at the Opera House."

Another tunnel testimony is from Clarence Woehlke who

worked for O.A. Haase Shoe Company on Main Street in the 1920s. Being fifteen or so at the time, he was told to deliver a package to the Athearn Hotel as he had done on many occasions.

Having a reputation for excellence, O.A. Haase repaired many shoes for performers from the Grand. When he inquired at the desk in the lobby of the Athearn that he had a package for a Miss Melius, the clerk said that she had just left and gone through the tunnel. For some reason Clarence said he knew right where to go. He said he went back by the alley and there was an opening to go under the sidewalk. It was just like daylight under there because of the glass cubicles in the roof of the sidewalk.

Clarence recalled meeting the famous vocalist, Lucile Melius. "I met her halfway under the sidewalk, gave her the package, turned and walked back. I assumed she was going through the tunnel to the Grand."

Julie said she talked to Roger Rose, a retired police officer about this same tunnel. Roger, a retired police officer and a fellow member of the Oshkosh Historical Society, told her at one of their meetings that he was in the tunnel.

He told Julie that it appeared that the Athearn side of the tunnel was closed before the Opera side of the tunnel. Rose told Julie he would patrol in the tunnel back in the days when cops had beats. Their duties included checking buildings to see if they were locked, and sometimes entering to see if anyone was in there that were not supposed to be.

Rose said that this was part of his regular beat and he often went in the tunnel and mentioned that toward the Athearn side there were a lot of folding chairs blocking the tunnel. As a result, he said, you couldn't enter the Athearn through the tunnel.

The controversy survives to this day.

Chapter Ten
Movie theaters

*T*he first motion picture theater that appeared in Oshkosh was the Bijou located on the east side of Main Street about where the old Peacock Restaurant and the Paper Tiger Book Store were located. By the time movie-going had become a habit for those with nickels and dimes in their pockets, other motion picture theaters appeared including the Lyric, the Colonial, and the Orpheum. Later the second and larger Bijou, which later became the Majestic, presented not only moving pictures but vaudeville as well. Down the street was the Rex which later became known as the Time Theater.

Bijou Theater

Other similar amusement houses sprang up on the south side of the river. Among the earliest were the Star and the Fay on 12th and Oregon across the street from each other. The Fay later became the

Mode in the 1930s. Another south side theater called the Family was located for a brief time on Oregon near 9th.

The movie audiences in these early theaters were able to follow the thought of the movie through the art of pantomime and printed subtitles.

Much of this would change in the 1920s when two of the finest movie theaters in the state – the Oshkosh and the Fischer (later known as the Strand or Raulf) were built. These two would change the landscape of theater-going in the city.

The Oshkosh Theater opened near the end of the silent-movie era in 1927. The theater was equipped with the Barton Organ that was manufactured by Dan Barton, an Oshkosh resident. The Barton organ music and its audio effects made up for a movie's lack of sound. A good organist could evoke horror, romance, excitement, joy and sadness as audiences watched the silent images on the screen.

The theater had a seating capacity of 2,000 which included a spacious balcony and a stage large enough for any vaudeville act, concert orchestra or other entertainment that was connected with the motion picture business.

When it opened on February 6, 1927, telegrams came from such well-known movie stars as Lon Chaney, John Gilbert, the Gish sisters, Ramon Navarro and Norma Talmadge. According to the *Northwestern*, "When the doors swing open to the new 'palace of wonders,' this city takes its rightful place among the other cities of the world theatrically."

I asked Marcille Simm, my 8th grade English teacher who grew up outside of Oshkosh and attended the local high school, if she would describe the theater in its earlier days.

"The Oshkosh was on Main Street, south of Church Street. It had plush carpeting, a plain lobby and two doors that opened from either side. There were sections of seats with plush carpeting down the aisles. The stage had velvet drapes and a moveable screen. An organ built by Barton's of Oshkosh played mood music for the movie. It must have taken a good organist to fit the music to the trend of the movie. At that time movies only had captions, no sound, so children had to be able to read as well as the adults."

"There were vaudeville acts presented often to the tune of the organ. It was presented before the movie was shown. Vaudeville at the Oshkosh Theater included acrobats, singers, skits, comedians and speakers."

Oshkosh Theater

On January 6, 1933 the talking movie "Silver Dollar" was shown at the Oshkosh. The movie had more than ordinary interest to those living in Oshkosh. The film was about the career of Senator H. A. Tabor of Colorado whose second wife was Elizabeth McCourt Doe, a member of a pioneer Oshkosh family.

Elizabeth or "Baby Doe," as she was known, was still living during the time of the showing. Penniless and living in a shack outside the town of Leadville, she was once called the Silver Queen of Colorado by virtue of being Horace Tabor's wife.

Soon after they married the two went on a spending spree

building an opulent opera house in Denver and bought an Italian villa. Tabor later became a U.S. Senator and had dreams of entering the White House with Baby Doe on his arm. But that was before their disastrous financial fall. Wiped out by unwise investments and by the Panic of 1893, Tabor soon died leaving his wife and their two daughters penniless. Reportedly on his deathbed he ordered his wife to hang on to the Matchless, a played-out silver mine filled with water. She managed to do that for almost four decades, struggling heroically against loneliness, poverty and heartbreak, and becoming one of the great legends of the American West.

Later on during the 1940s and '50s when I was a movie-goer, the Oshkosh, on many of those Saturday afternoons, would show double feature cowboy movies. Gene Autry, Roy Rogers and Hopalong Cassidy were the usual matinee performers.

Kids from every side of town came on those Saturday afternoons packing the theater yelling and rooting for their favorite cowboy. The cheering, the clapping, the jumping up and down is still there when I think back to those days.

One block up the street from the Oshkosh, when the theater was showing its first film, construction was underway on the new Raulf Hotel. The Raulf was meant to be a showplace for lodging, dining and entertainment. Along with bowling alleys in the basement, the hotel also had the city's newest and largest modern movie theater. When it opened it was named the Fischer. Later on the name changed to the Strand. It became the city's leading movie palace.

The Strand Theater

In an article in the *Northwestern* on November 23, 1927 it stated: "To describe the theater literally would necessitate superlatives that would not sound reasonable to the reading public. Yet almost anything that could be said of it would be justified and without exaggeration."

"It is doubtful if any city of this size can boast of a theater as elaborate and beautiful. Throughout the country there are some larger but none more artistic. Entering the auditorium of the theater is like being transported back 400 years to the days of old Spain. It's like stepping into a beautiful garden of a Spanish courtyard. Overhead silvery stars glisten and twinkle in a sky of Mediterranean blue. Around the walls and a series of arches that give the impression of an old courtyard wall covered with vines and shrubs beyond where you can glimpse far off mountains."

The newspapers description of the two theaters might appear to be an embellishment, but to many of us who had the opportunity of patronizing these two downtown theaters in the 1940s and '50s, we will never forget what once was.

The Oshkosh Theater closed in 1957 thirty years after its grand opening. It was an apparent victim of television. It was announced on August 2, 1960 in the *Northwestern* that the J.C. Penney Store plans to relocate a brand new department store building on the side of the defunct Oshkosh Theater.

The theater building was razed in the fall and the store was completed in the fall of 1961. The current Kitz & Pfeil is now the occupant of that site. The Strand or the Plaza Theater as it was known later closed in the mid-1970s.

There were two theaters to choose from on the south side of town and for ten or fifteen cents you could see a double feature, cartoons, coming attractions, a newsreel, and, if you chose the Star, a weekly serial as well. The Mode was the theater of choice when you wanted to be drawn into the story, to be caught up in the action, the suspense. To walk that one short block away to the quietness of the theater and experience another place in another time in a darkened place of make-believe, was my way of shutting out the outside world for four hours on those long-ago Sunday afternoons.

The Star, though, was the most fun because it was not as strictly supervised as the Mode. If you were in a mood to watch a good WWII flick or something else that had depth slightly below the surface, you chose the Mode. They didn't permit any noise there. But if you wanted to have fun, act like a kid, throw popcorn or jujus at someone two rows down, you went to the Star. And the Star showed serials.

The serials (we called them chapters) relied upon a much tested device for keeping suspense alive one weekend to the next and it seemed to always work. It was drama by installments. They were motion picture cliffhangers even in the literal sense. How many times did the stagecoach plunge over the cliff just as the episode ended? How many times did the wagon laden with burning hay crash into the ranch house killing the besieged hero, his girl companion and his faithful saddlemate? We knew the hero and those with him had escaped unharmed ready for the next episode adventure. Nevertheless, the nagging thought that this time they may not have escaped returned us to the Star the next Sunday, and the next, and the Sunday after that.

The Perils of Nyoka and its sequel, Jungle Queen, were two of my favorites. Nyoka was a lady Tarzan, swinging through the trees on vines battling fearlessly with diamond hunters and gorillas. But, unlike Tarzan, she was feminine and beautiful. And when she was captured and about to be tortured or harmed her boyfriend always came to the rescue. In a few of those episodes with a leap of faith and some imagination, I became that hero and the benefactor of Nyoka's favors.

But there was a downside to the Star beyond the insidious noise and rowdiness when you actually got caught up in the film's plot and its characters. The toilet facilities were in the basement. Rumor had it that rats roamed freely there so you either held it, or, if that was not possible, not take long doing what you had to do.

And then there was Charlie, a little boy in a man's body, who was a fixture on those Sunday afternoons. Charlie had difficulty distinguishing between make-believe and reality, and when he became immersed in what was happening on the screen, which seemed to be always, he would cry out, shout for the evil-doers to stop, bawl when a dog was run over by a stagecoach, cheer when Hoppy corralled the horse thieves, or when Wild Bill out-dueled the town bully, and clap loudly when the hero and his lady friend rode off into the sunset. It was a scene beyond belief to those of us too young to understand. So we were mean, real mean as kids can often be. Charlie often went home crying, not because of the roller coaster of emotions he experienced watching the movie. No, it wasn't that, sad to say, it was because of us; what was said; what we did.

I enjoyed most every kind of movie; musicals, westerns, adventures, war stories, films of most any description. And a few that I watched like Casablanca, A Tree Grows in Brooklyn and Grapes of Wrath stand out above most of the others. And if movies do indeed influence, mold, and shape, these three have done that for me.

Chapter Eleven
Stein's Mansion

*L*ike many growing up on the south side of town, I was unaware of this store-in-a-mansion that brought world-wide attention. There was little if any talk of Stein's at our house, at least none I remember. My mother simply did without as she skimped with the little money her husband brought home on payday. Providing food, clothing and shelter for her husband and six children were her main concerns. To think of shopping at the exclusive Stein's was something she, and many other women of working-class husbands, simply did not do or think of doing.

My interest in this long-ago women's finery started when I was writing the book, Oshkosh The Way We Were. Marcille Simm, my 8th grade English teacher, contributed a series of stories for the book, including one on Stein's. Her story piqued my interest, and when Dan Radig and I got together to search through his Oshkosh historic photograph collection for ideas for a book cover I said, when I saw the photo of this magnificent three-story mansion, Dan that's the one I want.

When I decided to write the story on this imposing structure that housed the most exclusive lady's finery in the Midwest, I tapped a few known sources including Janice Dibble, head of Reference and Adult Services at the Oshkosh Public Library who loaned out the booklet, Frank Stein Remembered, a booklet conceived by Gloria Miner, a former employee of Frank Stein & Company.

Mrs. Miner was joined by others, notably Jean Nelson, in acquiring information and artifacts of the Stein years. But it was Gloria Miner, secretary to Frank Stein from 1943 until the shop was destroyed by fire in 1947, who was the driving force in contacting fellow former employees and collecting their reminiscences. Mrs. Nelson remembered Stein's point of view of the customer. The text of the booklet was written by James Metz who was also the editor of the *entire project.*

There were other sources used including Oshkosh Northwestern *articles of October 2, 1947, March 30, 1951, June 5, 1953, October 23, 1997 and June 1, 2010, a Frank Stein Company promotional booklet designed and produced by the Miles Kimball Company in 1945, and a great deal of help from Gloria Suckow Miler, a fellow classmate whose aunt and grandmother worked there and, on occasion, stopped in to just look around.*

Thanks to each of these sources and to those who are still living to allow me to use their names and their stories.

"For many in Oshkosh it is not more than a memory. Countless others have never heard of it," was the opening statement in a 1955 *Northwestern* article written by Bruce Erdman.

"Frank Stein's swank, retail establishment was perhaps the only store in the world that was housed in a big rambling residence tastefully decorated and arranged. The Stein Shop looked more like a wealthy man's home than a store selling merchandise."

That elegant house on Church Street in which Frank Stein opened his world-famous shop was originally the palatial residence of George Gates, an official of the Diamond Match Company of Oshkosh. Mr. Stein, after giving it much thought, purchased the home at a public auction, remodeled it, and opened it for business in 1924.

It has been written that Stein devoted many years in refurbishing the interior with beautiful decorative trimmings that made the shop such a showplace attracting guests from all parts of the country. Mae Paterson, a world famous opera singer, once wrote: "I envy the women of Oshkosh and those for a hundred miles around, the luxury of this amazing store."

Stein, who was no stranger to this city, having grown up on the south side, first opened an exclusive ladies' ready-to-wear shop on Main Street in 1911. He then made what was considered an unwise and unprecedented decision thirteen years later by buying at auction the sixty-seven room Gates Mansion on Church Street several blocks away.

"I was thirty years old," he said. "I had a well-established business on Main Street. The future was not exactly discouraging but I was disgusted and bored with myself and my business. I decided to make everything on one roll of the dice, and I didn't much care if I won or lost."

Stein was concerned with the mounting cost of conducting business on Main Street, and the realization that the growing use of automobiles had changed living habits. The idea of transferring his entire ladies' wear store from a congested and tax expensive Main Street to a residential district began to make sense.

Rents and property taxes on Main Street were rapidly mounting at the time. Had Stein remained there it would, in his estimation, have been necessary to substantially increase his prices which he felt were already too high. He wanted a store where women could park their cars without hurrying and still sell the same high quality merchandise at a lower cost.

But as Erdman writes: "There was, however, no precedent to guide him. Nowhere in the world had anyone attempted to establish a store in a residence and combine a complete selection of women's wear with tea rooms for serving luncheons to its patrons."

Stein's plan was so new and revolutionary to what had always been considered good merchandising that his close friends discouraged it, and many old-time merchants questioned the possibility of success.

The house which became Stein's Lady's Apparel Shop boasted seven fireplaces with solid brass trim, beautiful woodwork of solid mahogany and onyx inlaid decorations, and plate glass and art glass from France. There was a hand carved stairway and a pipe organ between the first and second floors.

Stein's Women's Wear Store

Ladies could shop on several floors for fur coats, cloth coats, dresses, hats, lingerie, gifts and novelties while an organist provided background music from their huge pipe organ.

To further enhance the beauty of the building, Stein created an atmosphere similar to that of a private club or a friend's home. The uppermost thought of the saleswomen was never hurrying or urging a customer to buy, but to create a friend's "at home" atmosphere.

Carl Laemmle, former Oshkosh resident and Hollywood movie producer, said this about the store. "Duplicate this store in Paris, Mr. Stein, and you may draw on me up to one million dollars." And when a couturiere in Paris learned that her customer was from a town called Oshkosh, she exclaimed, "Ah, that is where you haves the magnificent store in a chateau."

The shop on Church Street was by no means exclusively for

women. Besides being able to assure male customers the kind of attention and expert assistance that made gift buying for the lady in his life a snap, Stein's actually had a room that was frequented by males. A second tearoom or luncheon area was opened in the basement of the fine old mansion. It was here that men often came together for socializing as the women did in the tea room on the first floor.

Gloria Miller when interviewed over coffee at Hardees on a warm Tuesday morning in August said: "My grandmother and aunt were employees at Stein's. Grandma Miller worked in the operations room doing alterations while my aunt was one of the buyers for Stein's, traveling to such destinations as Chicago and New York to buy the current fashions."

I asked if she ever entered Steins.

"Oh yes. When I would be going to a downtown movie I would stop in to see my grandmother and aunt. I often took a friend with me. It was my way of showing off, showing that I could go into Stein's that I had been there many times before."

"It was just so awesome. There was this wide, beautiful wooden stairway with hanging chandeliers, room enough for many to go up and come down, very much unlike our steep and narrow steps at home. Although Stein's was mainly a place for the well-to-do, it was so exciting for me to enter this beautiful mansion and not totally feel out of place. It was like a fairyland to me, coming from the Bloody 6th Ward."

Gloria grew up on 6th and Michigan.

In Gloria Miner's booklet, *Frank Stein Remembered*, many remembered this once beautiful shop.

Hazel Redford Drebus remembers the beautiful staircase and its lovely pipe organ. "It became a thrilling experience to be able to walk down that staircase with the beautiful organ music playing while modeling coats for Mr. Stein."

"My mother had accompanied me to Stein's for the purpose

of buying me a 'grown-up' coat. For some reason Mr. Stein noticed me as I pirouetted before the mirrors. He thought I would be a good teenage model. The year was 1938 and I was a sophomore in high school."

Lee Ann Christianson said: "I was born in 1941 but I do remember my mom taking me with her to shop at Stein's. A trip to Stein's was not just your ordinary shopping trip, it was an experience. Mom always dressed 'in her nines' and had me dressed equally as well. This was a place for even a little girl to be a lady."

"Mom and I sometimes sat in a 'tea room' or some such place. There were live models there that I thought were so beautiful. I was convinced in my child's mind that they must really be movie stars. That's how glamorous they were and how beautiful the décor was. Then sometimes I thought that those models must be very rich ladies who actually lived in the mansion."

Arleen Hansen Schroeder can still see the ladies fashion mansion located on Church Street in Oshkosh with its scrolled sign 'Stein's.' In her opinion it was the most beautiful architecture in Oshkosh.

"My first glance at this magnificent establishment was for an interview for employment. I was hired as the receptionist and met many people who were among the elite of Oshkosh and of other states. The customers were charmed at the beauty of the mansion."

Goldie Grabner, whose mother-in-law cleaned at Stein's, said: "If there was a sale my sister-in-law and I would check the clothes to see what we could get in our price range. We did buy a few things there that always made us feel so excited to wear because they were from Stein's which was considered a place for the rich to shop. We also felt rich wearing anything from there."

Gloria Miller, when asked if she bought anything at Stein's said, "Our family usually drew names for Christmas and most would go to Stein's to buy some relatively inexpensive item: a goblet, a piece of sterling silver, a dish, a cup, a candle holder, and occasionally one of those old-fashion martini glasses."

Stein's thought of everything. The store even carted the ladies home in the shops own station wagon after a long day of shopping and dining.

"Herman was the Stein's driver who picked people up at the train depot to shop at the store and then took them back in time to catch their trains wherever," recalled Pat Youngwirth who was seventeen when Stein's burned. "Herman would stand at the door and open it with a flourish for customers when he wasn't driving. He always had a good word and a smile for everyone."

Gloria Miler remembered that "Herman wore a black suit, white tie and hat. If you ordered a gift from Stein's Herman would drive up in the company's black car and deliver the purchased item. This was always a big deal for the customer as neighbors were impressed to see the Stein's car drive up realizing that this household shopped at the exclusive Stein's and of course, this would also bring a smile to the gift's beneficiary."

It all ended on the evening of September 30, 1947, Stein's caught fire and burned to a shell of its former self. The end occurred when the vapors from a faulty oil furnace built up, caught fire and burst forth in a loud explosion.

Carolyn Elmer said, "It was horrible! The heat was so intense – everything had melted including the pipes from the pipe organ, the fur off the coats – just hard skins were left hanging. I remember that day, September 30, 1947, as vividly as though it was yesterday."

Nearby residents said they heard a series of explosions, sounds similar to the backfire of a motor vehicle's exhaust shortly before the fire trucks arrived.

Ruth and Les Friday, who lived on the south side of town, reported the fire when driving by on Church Street, Mrs. Friday said she heard a noise like an explosion and saw the flames as they passed the shop. It was she who pulled the alarm box at the intersection of Jackson Drive and Church Street to alert the nearby fire station.

The headline on the front page of the *Northwestern* the following day read: $150,000 Damage Caused When Fire Sweeps Stein's Shop."

The story goes on to explain that the flames were caused by a faulty heating system resulting in heavy losses to the Woman's Dress and Gift Shop and Tearoom in the heart of the residential district.

"About ninety percent of the stock and sixty percent of the building was destroyed. This morning Mr. Stein, visibly suffering from shock, stated that the hand-carved solid mahogany woodwork, other precious wood fixtures and walls, and the manual pipe organ in the building were irreplaceably lost. The three story framed brick building and wood converted residential building bought by Mr. Stein 23 years ago at an auction was known throughout the nation as a showpiece of unique design."

"The large crowd that gathered was able to watch the firemen with ease due to the many searchlights playing on the building. Three policemen were on duty throughout the early morning and the remainder of the day to prevent looting. Mr. Stein was unable to state immediate plans for the future this morning. There are fifty-nine employees idled by the fire."

"At the time of the fire," Cerella Elmer said, "I was no longer employed at Stein's due to giving birth to our first child

Dennis, four weeks before. Althea (Mrs. Stein) called that night to tell me about the fire. The next morning she called again. Mr. Stein wanted me to come to see the devastation of his beautiful shop. Mr. Stein was seated in his car and watched my baby in his carriage while Althea took me into that once beautiful home."

Arlene Hanson Schroeder stated that "The memories of Stein's the morning of October 1, 1947 are sad. I lived in the country and was unaware of city happenings of the night before. When I got on the bus that morning with my bag lunch in hand, people started kidding me about going to work. One said that I was not going to work today because Stein's burned down last night. Of course I didn't believe her."

"As I neared Stein's my heart sank. I could see Stein's unique shop was no longer white, and the exquisite wonder of beauty which I loved was gone. The building was black and smoldering. Statues that had once graced the porch were blackened by smoke. The grand lantern posts were melted, the lights had gone out from Stein's forever. Tears ran down my cheeks as I walked down the once scenic driveway to the back of the store. I was thinking of the excellence this attractive building held and would no longer hold, for the fire had claimed her."

A reporter for the *Northwestern,* when reviewing the story of the fire some four years later, wrote: "There was a tragic blow in the cold night of September 30, 1947. A faulty boiler started a fire which destroyed sixty percent of the building's interior and ninety percent of the stock in a matter of a few hours. Mr. Stein, who often referred to his store as a 'beautiful lady,' stated so aptly the next day: 'The beautiful lady is an old hag today.' There were tears in his eyes as he said it."

A few days later the Oshkosh paper reported: "There will be a void in the downtown area as a once-famed structure will be erased from the city's visage. The former Stein's Shop which was known in the entire Midwest area as a women's fashion center in an unusual setting was housed in the structure at 12 Church Street which is being dismantled almost piece by piece."

An attempt was made shortly before Frank Stein's death to sell the structure to the city without success. The property was soon razed and the Krambo Food Store, that adjoined the property, bought it and made it into a parking lot.

The Stein property is now the site of the City's Safety Building.

Chapter Twelve
Taverns and other Drinking Establishments

They were the social centers of Oshkosh, the meeting places in the '40s and '50s. Others might make a case for the churches, but in the eyes of those still grubbing for wages and those of us growing into adulthood, it was the tavern.

There were no shortage of taverns in the city of 40,000 – 117 by one count. Most were within walking distance of anyone with a thirst for a taste of barley or simply a need to get out and be with the boys. Though taverns were no longer the sole refuge of the male specie, there were still a few not willing to address the social changes that free thinkers believed were long overdue.

Utechts, on 5th and Ohio, across the street from the Hour Tavern, still carried on the traditions and tastes of the working man's turn-of-the-century saloon. It was a small walk-up where you could belly up to the bar for a shot of booze and a glass of beer. With no bar stools, no seating of any kind, and only one toilet facility, it was no place for the fairer sex, the occasional drinker, or the highball and martini crowd. The real drinkers, the two-fisted ones, who put down 15 cents for a small shooter and the 10 ounce of glass of beer were the ones that made Utechts their second home.

A 1986 *Oshkosh Northwestern* article tells us about this south side establishment. The story's headline read: "For Sale, Utecht's steeped in Oshkosh Tavern History." Paul Srubas, a writer for the paper, tells us about this turn-of-the-century tavern.

You could call it the passing of an era, but it's only an old tavern that's up for sale, and an old barkeep who's about to retire.

Utecht's Tavern, 413 Ohio Street, Oshkosh, is one of those places you could enter almost any time of the day to find a half dozen men in work clothes drinking shots and beers. The conversation is always gruff, often coarse, and occasionally obscene.

Usually there's a cigar burning somewhere, and maybe a football game is on the tube on the wall. The TV is probably being ignored as customers, not actively involved in cards or a conversation, are usually busy staring into the depths of their beer glasses.

On a certain Thursday, at 9 o'clock in the morning, exactly a dozen men patronized the place. Some of them are bellied up to the bar with half-consumed beers before them, while others are involved in a raucous card game at a couple of the tables.

Stan Werner, Utecht's bartender since 1949, is rushing from customer to customer pouring out shots and beers with all the haste, nervousness and eagerness-to-please of a new employee. He is a trimly built man of 62 with glasses and a hoarse voice.

"I got out of the Navy, worked at the Wisconsin Axle for five years, and then they asked me if I'd tend bar. I've been here ever since. Now I want to retire so they said they'd sell it. They told me I'd have a job as long as I wanted it."

Werner's very accommodating boss and Utecht's owner is Jane Ehrenhardt, who acquired the bar four or five years ago from Russ Ehrenhardt, who acquired It from his uncle, George Utecht. The tavern has been in the same family for more than 80 years.

It's the kind of bar for men who like to walk in and have drink set before them without their having to order. A customer walks in and sits and Werner pours him a beer and double shot, then fetches him a can of snuff without a word being spoken.

"You've got guys that have been coming here for 50, 60 years and now I'm waiting on their sons," Werner said. He spoke of one man who had been coming to the tavern for 74 years, a man who started coming at the age of 6. "Rules" were somewhat slack 74 years ago."

This place is steeped in history – typical tavern history, that is Utecht's was one of those Oshkosh taverns famous for the old tradition of "rushing the pail," wherein people would bring in pails to buy beer.

"They'd bring in a pail and put lard around the edge to kill the foam so they'd get more beer. It was 25 cents a pail. They'd rush in and rush out so that's why it was called 'rushing the pail.' That was before my time. That was in your late '30s. The police weren't so bad then, so you could send your son."

Also Utecht's history is its policy of having no women in the place. Some say women were refused admittance, but Werner says they were merely discouraged from entering. "They were afraid to come in," he said. "It was known just as a man's place."

"Women were discouraged from entering by such ploys as making them stand – the tavern had no barstools. There was no juke box, no mixed drinks and no women's restrooms. They could go upstairs or across the street but if they used the men's, their husband would watch the door."

The place maintained its style for a good many years. Women would drop their husbands off for a quick drink and, while the man of the house was inside quenching his thirst, his wife would wait outside in the car. The more chivalrous husbands would occasionally bring drinks outside for their wives.

Traditions soon began to crumble when one woman began bringing her own barstool so she wouldn't have to stand at the bar. "She kept it in the back room," says Werner.

"More and more women began coming in. Eventually in 1962 the place was remodeled to keep up with the times. Things changed. We got a women's bathroom, put in a parking lot. We had to get bar stools. . . But you've got to keep up with the times."

Here Werner grows sort of quiet, reflective and buys me a beer.

"I liked it the old way, but we had to go with the changes or you'd be lost because of the overhead - gas, water, lights - that or raise prices. We didn't get the high class trade, always the regular working-class trade. All those changes are good. It increased our business."

Stan Werner's son, Lee, told me recently that he helped his dad at the tavern when he was young.

"I remember no bar stools, no dice boxes, no pool table. If you wanted to play a game it was "Screwy Louie" a form of "Crazy Eight." There were five bar stools in the back of the tavern but out of sight. And there was no women's bathroom until they remodeled in the 1960s. If a woman had to go she had to go across the street to the Hour. They didn't refuse women."

"If you were in there between three and six they were three deep at the bar. Utecht's was the most convenient tavern for the workers to have their shot and beer. And when they entered, each nearby factory – Rockwell, Paine's, the Foundry, Diamond Match - had its own place in the barroom. They would come in after work. It was a place where they could stand and talk, cash their checks on Friday. It was very much unlike the Hour where they had bar stools and served food."

"My dad got there every morning at six. He did everything

to get the bar ready for the first customers. There were some customers waiting at the back door when he arrived as they had just got out of work and needed a drink or two before heading home."

"When they remodeled in the '60s, the government required them to put in a women's bathroom. At that time guys were bringing in their wives especially after a wedding reception or some type affair where they were together."

"When some of these factories were laying off or closing, changes had to occur if taverns like Utecht's were to stay in business. Besides opening the tavern to women, they began to hold raffles on Saturday and Sunday mornings. They raffled off things they couldn't sell and guys thought they were getting a bargain."

There were more than a few taverns during the 1940s and '50s that served the underage crowd. Rumor had it the owners paid the cops to look the other way. Tad's Bar, Hour Tavern and Leroy's Bar were among those south side drinking establishments that catered to these new customers.

The Hour Tavern, with its booths along the outer walls, a dance floor in the middle, a jukebox playing the top forty, and a kitchen serving inexpensive food, was the favorite place for the not-yet-21 crowd.

Witzke's on 17th and Repp's on Oshkosh Avenue were long established places on the south side as well. They were primarily shot and beer and card playing establishments. And there were taverns on the north side that were noted to serve the underage crowd as well.

Jerry's Bar and Trail's End are two notable examples of taverns that existed a long time in the city.

Jerry's is the oldest tavern in town. It is estimated that the building has been "standing" since 1858. The oldest records of the building were lost in one of the legendary Oshkosh fires but this neighborhood bar survived and eventually became the headquarters for the Otter Street Fishing Club and a place for customers to sit, play cards, socialize, and enjoy tipping back a glass of beer.

Marty Wesenberg, who I interviewed some years back, said Charlie Rahr, from Rahr's Brewery, talked his grandfather, who was tending bar at the East End Tavern on the corner of Rosalia and Ceape at the time, into renting this place in 1911. "Charlie said he would set him up. He brought down a back bar, a front bar, a liquor cabinet, an icebox and a variety of other furnishings from some of the uptown taverns he owned to get him started. Rahr Brewery, like Oshkosh and Peoples, owned many of the taverns in Oshkosh."

Marty said there were no woman toilets when he started. "My dad told me that years ago you didn't see women in the bar room. In some taverns there were family rooms where husbands and wives and their children could sit, drink some beer or pop, and enjoy tavern food. But not in the bar proper."

"Years ago the tavern was a poor man's club. Our customers couldn't afford to be a Mason, a country club member or whatever, but he could come in with a handful of nickels, drink some beer and meet up with friends."

"To have a neighborhood tavern is like having a big family. You see the guys every day. I see my sister once a month, my brother who lives two doors down every two weeks. I laugh a lot but I cry a lot too. When there's a death, divorce or some such tragedy in the families it hurts. I think the owner of any neighborhood tavern would say that."

Many working men in the 1940s and '50s cashed their checks in taverns. Marty said his dad was one of many tavern owners who kept a lot of cash on hand on paydays. They were glad to do this as most everyone, after having their checks cashed, would toss down a few drinks before heading home.

And it was not uncommon for customers to put drinks on the tab during the week and clear their bills on Friday.

"Most every customer was from the neighborhood. Most taverns in the city back then were neighborhood bars. And at one time there were over one hundred and thirty such places in the city. Once you established yourself and treated them right, the kids and grandkids would follow."

Scott Engel is one of the new owners of the bar. Scott represents the 6th generation of Wesenbergs to own the tavern.

Scott is reaching out to others in the city through various promotions. He has, according to Marty, nine softball teams, four bowling teams, and a handball, soccer and basketball teams.

'Scotty is now the one who makes the decisions."

I sensed that Marty knew that businesses had to keep up with the times; that change was often necessary; that it was easier for the young to do this. Perhaps Marty thought back when his dad owned the tavern and his reluctance to accept the changes Marty often proposed. Maybe those thoughts helped to salve wounds inflicted on men like Marty, who are caught up in places not of their time.

Trail's End, located on the corner of Merritt and Broad, was an excellent location to have a tavern. It was located in the 4th Ward, populated by beer-loving European immigrants. Across the street was the Chicago and Northwestern Railroad Depot. Passengers who got off the train would immediately see the sign for Oshkosh beer.

Along the same railroad tracks were Dumphy Boats and Carver Dairy products. Workers from these and other nearby factories, including my dad, would usually stop for beer when the work day ended. All sorts of people entered these doors located in this blue-collar district. It was not only a "shot and beer" place but also a place for families to gather for a meal.

The tavern got its start in 1892 with a bar and two bowling alleys. Twenty years later the alleys were later converted into a dining room. The tavern was purchased by the Oshkosh Brewing Company in 1896 because it was a popular drinking spot.

Prohibition started with the passage of the 18th Amendment making it illegal to drink, sell and manufacture alcoholic beverages so the saloon, and others in the city, evolved into soda emporiums selling soft drinks and sandwiches.

But that was never going to cut it in Oshkosh.

The place was in financial trouble when Bill Vandenberg bought the business in 1923. Vandenberg put his own name – Van's – on the sign and put booze in the soda cups.

In the spring of 1923 Vandenberg, his wife and two daughters moved into the house connected to the tavern. The story of how Vandenberg concealed the liquor trade during Prohibition was told by his granddaughter.

"There was a doorway that connected the house and the bar. The patrons would have a special knock for different alcoholic beverages. My great grandmother ran the door from inside the house and would serve the drinks from there."

It was one of the better speakeasy setups in Oshkosh. But it wasn't bootleg booze that made Van's famous. It was the special secret sauce on the hot dogs that drew people far and wide.

Among the new rules established when Prohibition was repealed in 1933 was a law forbidding a tavern owned by a beer company to sell only their patron's beer. The monopolistic practice by Rahr's, People's and Oshkosh no longer existed. It wasn't long before the local brewing companies began selling taverns they owned.

In 1960 the Oshkosh Brewing Company were selling their remaining properties and Bob Winkelman bought Van's in

1984 and named it Trail's End. He is still the owner today.

Like Jerry's Tavern, there was no way Trail's End could conceal its age. The floor slopes and the bar show plenty of wear.

Although not strictly a tavern, Club 41, a night club, was located just north of Murdock across from the fairgrounds. They named it Club 41 because in those days US 41 went right through Oshkosh on its way from Milwaukee to Green Bay.

The new club was the finest in Oshkosh at the time. They did well with a large dance floor and big parking lot. They had a dance band every night. In later years Joe Weisheipl and his band, featuring his brother Corky on the trumpet, played there on weekends. Corky played with many of the big bands of those days.

After WWII it was sold to the Knights of Columbus Club. The club featured weddings, banquets, and other affairs like high school reunions which our high school class celebrated there some years ago.

On June 15, 1940, the Magnet Bar at 519 Main Street in Oshkosh became the first tavern in the state of Wisconsin to be issued a beer-only license. Teenagers in Oshkosh and surrounding communities finally had a legal place to drink beer.

The Magnet was at the vanguard of what would become a memorable Wisconsin phenomenon – teenage beer bars. These were places where people 18-20 years of age could enjoy their brew of choice in an atmosphere unspoiled by hard liquor.

After Prohibition, Wisconsin reserved a local option allowing municipal government s to set the age for legal beer drinking. The local option hadn't been exercised until Frank Hayes took out a class B liquor license and convinced Oshkosh officials he could run a clean-cut beer and billiard hall. By July of 1940 Wisconsin's first beer bar was in business.

But it didn't start out at The Magnet and it didn't start on Main Street. The Magnet began as the Playdium on the corner of Main on Washington Boulevard. The proprietor, Frank Hayes, didn't tolerate rude behavior in his beer bar. Fighting, swearing and loud noises were not welcome at the Playdium.

In 1950 Hayes moved his bar to its present site on Main Street, but kept the beer-only status. It didn't take long before other beer bars in the city, namely, Hergerts, Arvs, Ralo, the Keg, and the Loft opened their doors to this eager but mostly inexperienced crowd.

These were drinking establishments only. No Friday night fish fries here. And with the exception of the people on duty, no adult supervision either. When the adults did come, it was usually the police breaking up fights or arresting someone who had too much to drink.

The young, with alcohol in their veins, were not always able to mute their tendencies to protect, defend, or simply contain their eagerness to fight. Sexual tension and male machismo were the usual culprits. Poor Ma and Pa Hergert, an older couple who decided to give up the ice cream business, opened a beer bar in the basement of their home and had to contend with the pushing and shoving, the fist fights, the scattering of stools and chairs when the testosterone levels got too high.

Among other things beer bars served was a central casting place for the unattached. The array of choices was far greater than they were in the neighborhood bars many of us clung to. Although the under-21 crowd was not an untapped resource for the tavern owners, it had not, before the passage of this law, been fully addressed either.

Oshkosh, as you would expect, soon became the destination for those in neighboring communities to come and get their fill of beer before taking to the highways and returning to their dry hometowns.

In 1959 Winnebago County was attempting to enact a law that would fix the beer age at 21 county-wide. They failed but four years later the Oshkosh Common Council decided it was time to abandon the local option of beer bars in Oshkosh, and once again alcoholic beverages became the privilege of those over 21.

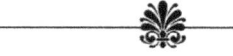

Chapter Thirteen
Fishing shanties along the Fox

*F*ish shanties once lined the south shore of the Fox River in Oshkosh all the way to its mouth were the Pioneer Inn was once located. Fishing was a serious business back then. It was largely done at night when fish preferred to travel. Men and some women would line the south shore of the river and fish from the embankments, under bridges, from boats and from fishing rafts or shanties. The fishing lanterns lit up the river from the embankments of the Morgan Company all the way to the railroad bridge.

The fishing shanties were also used extensively for social purposes – card games, family meals and "tossing a few down." They were used as summer social centers for the average to low-income person or families. Being out over the water was a big attraction as well because of the coolness, the views and the activity around you.

These fishing structures provided a way for a person to support themselves through fishing as well as being able to associate and interact with others. This was especially important during hard times when out-of-work people could go to them and get their mind off their troubles. Recreation at a bar, pool hall, or theater was often out of the question for those who could not afford it.

When I decided to find out more about those who still cling to the culture of the river, I met one of the owners at the Farmers Market on a Saturday morning at my book stall. After introducing himself, Tom De Roos asked if I would be interested in doing a story on the fishing shanties in Oshkosh.

There are few in Oshkosh aware of their presence today. They hide well even if you catch a glimpse of the few remaining as you cross the Wisconsin Avenue Bridge from the north. The new river walk on the south shore that extends under the bridge and continues to the terminus of Michigan Street by the water is an easier way of their discovery. And if you do take that short walk and survey the scene, *you may be able to take yourself back those many years when fishing along the banks of the river was a way of life.*

About a month later I took that river walk stroll once again and met with Tom and his wife, and Gerald Tollard. After introductions were made, Tom asked me to take a seat in his shanty.

They were both eager to get their story out.

"It's a way of life for us," recounted Gerald who was the previous owner of the shanty. "That's how we learned to fish. This shanty and the experience on the river were passed down from my father's and grandfather's time. We grew up here with our family. My kids grew up here as well. Now it's more of a social thing than it was during my grandfather's time, less so my father's time. We have friends down for fish fries. We fry whatever we catch – catfish, white bass, perch or walleye. Most who live in the city don't have this type of opportunity."

"And we think it's a good way to keep our kids out of trouble. When we grew up in the '50s and '60s, we were hell-raisers like many others in the neighborhood, but we stayed out of real trouble because the bunch of us could come down here in the summer to fish and just while a way time on the river."

"Two of my brothers and I owned this shanty before it was sold to Tom who is a relative of ours. We wanted it to stay in family. One of my brothers lives in Marathon, Wisconsin and the other is a machinist who works long hours. I later got sick and couldn't keep up with all the maintenance that was required."

"I've had this shanty for about five years now," Tom commented. "I started down here when I was about ten. I grew up in the Westhaven area. I would ride my bike here twice a day, every day, morning and evening between the ages of twelve and seventeen. That's how much I loved it here."

A few of the remaining fishing shanties

"There are some in this city who claim these shanties are an eyesore. I've been told by numerous people, especially those who live in this area, that if it ever comes down to signing a petition or anything of the sort they would support us. I would think as long as we keep the shanties up and keep them clean, I don't think anyone should have a problem."

This essentially is the reason I was invited to tell their story. They wanted the citizens of Oshkosh to know the opposition they were facing by those who are the city's decision makers.

I asked if there were any municipal directives regulating shanties.

"We have never seen anything in writing," remarked Tom, "whereby we cannot do this or that. We do know that we are not able to rebuild though. We try to keep it clean and updated. We do no hell-raising with parties and such. And we try to be respectful of the river and of the nearby community."

"We don't hear anything directly from the city as far as regulations are concerned. When we do on occasion find out something we either read it in the *Northwestern* or someone attending the City Council meetings might tell us of a discussion that affected us."

"We try to keep it clean down here out of respect for the environment. We don't dump garbage and we try to maintain our shacks as best we can."

"Years ago," Gerald added, "few of these shanties had toilet facilities. The waste went right into the river. That's not done anymore. When the shanties were first built back in the 1920s and '30s a number of the shacks used the river for this purpose. That no longer exists."

Tom took over at this point.

"There was a meeting this past spring (2013) when a number of the shanty owners went down to a meeting hosted by the local Historical and Archaeological Board because one of the Board members was pitching the idea of getting rid of the shanties. He claimed that the shanties had no historical value and were an eyesore along the river."

"When you talk to people in this area whose families used to have a shanty," said Gerald, "it was a way of life, part of their culture that was passed from one generation to the next. And once these are gone that part of our town's history is gone."

"Oshkosh on the Water is a good share of our history. The lumber and saw mills, the rolling logs, the river boats, and I might add, the fishing shanties were all a part of the history on the river."

"You can see the many photos of Paine's with the floating logs but if you visit the museum you won't find pictures of the many boat houses along the river. Despite the fact there are only seven of these shanties left, there was a time, not long ago, when there were about twenty in this area alone."

"People can come down here, look around and realize what Oshkosh was like years ago before it was built up."

It was strongly suggested during these interviews that the City Council, the City Administration, and the Oshkosh Historical and Archaeological Society wanted to shut down their way of life, to close the shanties. It wasn't difficult to pick up their sense of urgency that they were being ambushed from above, from those who might have the authority to eliminate their way of life.

"Years ago, somewhere in the 1980s, the city wanted us to leave here. The city posted bulletins on our boathouses when we were not present, stating that we must leave by December 4th of that year. When we came down here and saw the postings and discovered the electricity was cut off at the poles, we also saw that someone or some group of people came down and broke in our boat houses and took whatever they felt was salvageable."

Who did this?

"We don't know, although the city was at fault for cutting off our electricity and for the posting of signs on the boathouses without prior notice. Vandalism was going on like crazy down here and it was hard to keep track of all the stuff that was carried away or damaged."

"Here's the other thing that happened. While we were fighting this, a boathouse burned down. A week later another burned down next to us. The wall of this shanty (I'm looking as he's pointing towards the wall in front of me) was completely burned off and the roof and ceiling had to be rebuilt. So we had to put a tin roof on it so it wouldn't leak."

"We owned another small boat house in back of this one and when we came back after the posting we discovered the back door was kicked in and when entering we found a pile of burned rags on the floor. Apparently someone was also trying to torch that one as well. They – whoever they were – did torch it later and ruined the back part of the boathouse so we were forced to tear it down and remove the pilings."

Tom said he recently received a letter from the City Manager addressed to the City Council stating that there is a new shanty being built on the river. The City Manager asked the Council what they intended to do about this.

"No one from the city came down to investigate or to talk with us. The truth of the matter was the shanty in question sunk. We could have just allowed it to sink and lay on the bottom of the river. But we thought the best course was to pull it out."

Both of you are giving me the feeling that the city is working against your best interests and interests of the city's river history.

"Well first of all, the city will not allow us to improve our shacks on the outside hoping the shacks deteriorate to the point we will no longer want to stay here. Last year we asked the city to put buoys throughout the river and it was shot down. They don't want a speed limit down here. Tourism is wrecking the shoreline and slowly deteriorating our shanties when these big boats are allowed to race up and down the river. Look at the Plaza down there. They had to replace most of the concrete lining their shores."

Why do you cling to this way of life?

"Because we grew up with this," Gerald said with a sense of urgency. "It's passed along from one generation to the next and that traditions and family heritage we want to continue. It's more like I'm doing it to honor my father and grandfather and because I love it down here."

I asked how long this particular shanty has been here.

"It seems forever but it I think it was built sometime before the Depression. This boathouse however has undergone changes. It was larger back then than it is now. But over the years it deteriorated a bit so my grandpa and father and his brothers fixed it up, remodeled it. The pilings had to be reworked to accommodate a smaller boathouse. All of the boathouses have been here for at least sixty to seventy years. This shanty has had five generations living here."

It would be fair-minded for each of us to remember that fishing shanties once lined the south shore of the Fox River in Oshkosh all the way to its mouth where the Pioneer Inn was once located.

Tom Hansen, a friend and a former DNR employee, told me that the shanty owners may have had leases from the railroad or perhaps were just squatters. But after the Pioneer Inn was built they, other than a few, were history."

Getting back to the interview I mentioned that one of the arguments I've heard that runs against your interests is that the city provides services but you pay no property taxes.

"Yes, that's true," said Tom. "The police did come down here as well as the fire department years ago because of the fore-stated vandalism. But that's all the services the city provided. We're taxpayers as both of us own land property in the city. I haven't been to the Council meetings to argue this point. I try to stay away from those meetings primarily because it gets too heated."

Gerald mentioned that the city came down a number of years ago and appraised these boathouses.

"We told them we would be more than willing to pay our share of taxes. I don't know if they were down here to find a reason to kick us out or what they may have had on their minds. They found out later they could not do it legally because these shacks are over the water and not on land. It was in our estimation that this was the city's idea to find a reason to get us out of here. We never heard another word about that."

"One of the difficulties for those who want to close us

down is that our shacks are over federal waters. If you move these boathouses you have to remove all the pilings in the river as well. The Corp of Engineers has to make that decision because our shacks set above the water."

Although they both feel an ongoing and intimate relationship with these shanties, its history and culture, Gerald, perhaps because of his family's history on the river, is the one that is most easily riled by the turn of events.

"This way of life is not our livelihood as it was for our grandparents and to a lesser degree for some of our parents. My grandfather fished to put food on the table as did many others during the time of the Great Depression. That's one reason they built these shacks. It was another way of making a living. We no longer do that because we don't have to. We simply enjoy fishing. Now and then we have a fish fry and invite friends and family here. When you get older you no longer see your friends as much as you would like. So we invite them down here when we have a good crop of fish. It's a nice get-together."

Is this way of life losing its appeal?

"The reason it might have lost its appeal to some is that some of the former owners got sick of fighting City Hall. There were a number of shacks that burned down and some allowed them to collapse in the water. We're the ones that have to pull this crap out. We had to come down here with dumpsters and pick things up when this occurred."

"Robbie and Sonny Demler used to own a shack over there (pointing towards the Wisconsin Avenue Bridge). Some of the shanty owners moved on thinking it wasn't worth fighting for. Many of this same south side family still come down and sit on the dock and reminisce."

What might be lost if these shanties were no longer here?

"Family tradition would be lost. All my relatives that are

still living that's all they seem to talk about. Many of them still come down here with their grandsons and tell them about the past. The shanties keep the kids out of trouble and we get them started in fishing. Would you rather have them hanging out in the park breaking up the bathrooms and destroying everything? Look at Menomonie Park. They had to place a curfew there. We never had a curfew in town before. We have nothing for the kids to do anymore."

Gerald is still speaking.

"When I was younger you had park dances, Lourdes had dances, the Rec building had dances during the summertime. Kids always had something to do – fishing, swimming, going down to the playgrounds. And we had public swimming beaches then. The beach at Menomonie Park is now an eyesore for the city. They used to have lifeguards, showers, flags and a T dock out there. Now nothing. You take everything away from the kids and you wonder why you have a bunch of teenagers not having anything constructive to do."

"The fishing docks were also taken away. The old Foster-Lothman dock at the end of Minnesota Street on the river was always filled with fisherman."

After spending time with Gerald and Tom and listening, if somewhat briefly, to one who has a seat on the Historical and Archaeological Board, it wasn't difficult for this writer, who grew up on the side of town that too often distrusted the business community and the town's doers and shakers, to side with the remaining few who want to preserve the culture of their inheritance.

Chapter Fourteen
World War II

Unlike wars since, Americans at home sacrificed as well as those serving our country overseas. By the end of World War II, more than 12 million American soldiers had joined or were drafted into our armed forces. Widespread rationing occurred during the war. Families, for example, were given coupons to purchase sugar based on the size of their families. They could not buy more than their coupons would allow. Rationing covered more than just food – it also included goods such as shoes and gasoline.

Some items were just not available. Silk stockings made in Japan were replaced by the new synthetic nylon stockings. No automobiles were produced from February, 1943 until the end of the war so industries could start manufacturing war specific items. Many women entered the workforce to help make munitions and implements of war. These women were nicknamed "Rosie the Riveter" and were a central part of this country's success in defeating the Axis Powers.

The following stories are from the author, three of his boyhood friends and from their 8th grade English teacher who experienced the war in different ways.

Together with the lingering effects of the Depression, World War II was the natural state of affairs during the early part of the 1940s. I still remember that most every evening on our new Philco console, we would gather around and listen to Gabriel Heatter declare at the end of his broadcast: "And the sky over England is not yet in Hitler's hands."

Shortly into the war our mother received ration books and tokens. When she went to buy meat, butter, sugar and shoes later on, she needed to hand over ration stamps or dime size tokens along with money to buy the item.

Most everyone planted a vegetable garden. It provided fresh and inexpensive food and it was patriotic as it saved canned vegetables for our soldiers overseas; the bigger the garden, the greater the patriotism. In our neighborhood the Hielsbergs were the most patriotic.

No one was immune from the war. It was in our comics, in our movies, in our songs. The radio was filled with it. Most evenings my parents listened to Edward R. Murrow from London and Gabriel Heatter in his New York studio updating their listeners on the progress of the war.

Wartime in the forties had a feeling of its own. Unlike wars since, World War II had a home front. Civilians felt the war and fought it too. They fought it by working long hours in war industries. They fought it at the dinner table, with the cars they no longer drove and in the things they did without. They fought it by buying war bonds, by growing Victory Gardens, by conserving and salvaging things previously thrown away. They fought it in their minds as patriots, and they fought it in the songs they sang. The deeply felt a sense of loyalty and responsibility to get the job done.

To help finance the war effort we bought war stamps that we pasted in a United States Savings Bond booklet. When the booklet was full - $18.75 worth – it could be exchanged for a $25 war bond. This piecemeal fashion of loaning money to the government allowed even poorer families to help save a soldier's life.

There were air raid warnings and blackouts during the early years of the war. The roof of the First National Bank on Main Street was used by civil defense workers as a lookout for spotting enemy aircraft. I'm not sure if any were spotted but I do remember Mother turning off the lights and pulling down the shades in our living room during that first city-wide blackout. The sirens blared and the seriousness that filled the air made the moment eerie to a 7 year old.

Kids helped too. Bob "Honey" Hielsberg and I, when we were trying to scrape up some spending money, went door-to-door asking for old newspapers, cardboard, rags, and metals and then took them down to Block Iron and Salvage or to Pumps on Tenth Street by the river. On a good day each of us might walk home with 50 or 60 cents in our pockets.

Wayne Gruhlke said that he was unaware at a young age the impact the war had on families that had a son, a father or some relative fighting overseas and also trying to adapt to the culture of scarcity.

I was five when we went to war. It was actually a time of prosperity for me and my buddies. I was a "junker," a term used and glorified during the next four years. A more appropriate name might have been scavenger for that is what we did.

The War Department put out a call to all junkyards and towns throughout the country to donate to the war effort. Raw materials such as copper, lead, zinc, brass, paper, rags, aluminum and tin cans were needed in large quantities. Special drives for these materials were held periodically.

When a few of us realized we could search the piles of booty deposited on city curbs to be picked up later by the city, we would simply rummage through all the junk and take the "good stuff" to either Pumps or Block Iron and Salvage along the river on 10th Street. After a few of these transactions, we felt the owners of these two south side junkyards were shorting us on the weight thus depriving us of the payout we felt we deserved. Unfortunately for us, the weighing scale was inside the building and admittance was not given to a couple of kids putting loose change in their pockets.

We also searched through the garbage at the South Side

Dump soon after the garbage trucks dumped their cargo. Anything we found that would bring a few coins in our pockets was fair game. We never made a lot of money but always enough to buy candy and get to an occasional movie.

The local Chief Oshkosh Brewery was also a source of pocket money. I'm no longer sure of the number, but you could get a 25 cent U.S. Savings stamp for turning in about 500 bottle caps. After you filled up a savings bond booklet of stamps that were worth $18.75, you could go to the bank and get a $25 U.S. Savings Bond. We dropped this venue after being told that the bond could not be cashed for a number of years. We were probably the only kids in the city that hated to see WWII end, a war that later on in our adult years took on a totally different meaning.

Tom Hansen added this to enhance our understanding of Oshkosh during the war.

During the early years of the war we would take our ration stamps and tokens to two nearby grocery stores on Bowen Street to shop. The rationing of food was a constant reminder we were at war.

To ease the situation there was a "Toy Loan" on Ceape Street where you could play with and check out toys similar to checking out books from the public library.

I can also recall a family gathering around the console radio in our living room that may have been the announcement of the Pearl Harbor attack.

I also had four uncles that served in the war. One was a marine who saw action in Midway, Guadalcanal and Bouganville. Another was with the 32nd in New Guinea and a third with the army in Europe. Another served as a reserve officer in a prison camp in Texas. All had interesting stories to tell.

Ken Steinert said his recollection of the first Sunday in December of 1941 is a little hazy.

I do recall that our family went to church that Sunday like we did every Sunday. When we returned home my parents, who heard some people talking about Pearl Harbor in church, were keeping a tight ear to the radio. Later that day we visited relatives and there was much grown-up talk about an attack somewhere out in the Pacific Ocean. Although this day changed the life of my family and lives of many of my relatives, as it did for many across America, it had little impact on a 6 year old growing up on the south side of Oshkosh.

Life for me went on pretty much as usual. There were no computers or cell phones then. Everything moved slower and we created our own games and did most things outside. Our neighborhood covered 11th street from Jefferson School west to South Park. There must have been 15 of us under the age of 10 in the neighborhood. It was a great time to be a kid.

The carnival came to town each summer and set up their rides and game tents on the corner of 11th and Ohio. These grounds are now occupied by the Gelhar Gas Station and the old Piggly Wiggly building. A few of us would hang out with the smart-talking "carny" guys and hear things that were probably inappropriate for our young ears. Occasionally we might get a free ride on the Merry-Go-Round.

Winter was filled with good times. Sledding, building snow forts, and ice skating were the staples of youth. But summer was when the real fun began. We rode bikes, played cowboy and Indians with homemade toy guns made out of scraps of wood and played baseball in front of our house on 11th Street. After supper, all the kids in the neighborhood would gather for a game. Sides were chosen and bases were marked with a rock or a board. We played until the street lights came on unless the game was cut short because of an argument over a close call.

If the owner of the ball was involved in the fracas and was on the wrong end of the call, he might take his ball and go home. When this happened, as it often did, we would finish off the day with a rousing game of Kick-the-Can.

While we enjoyed these good times, our parents kept us insulated from the details of the war. There was no television so any visual we saw came from *Life Magazine* or from the "Eyes and Ears of the World" news reel when we went to see a movie at the Mode Theater.

These were stressful times for my parents. Three of my dad's brothers were in the armed services. The weekly *Shop-O-Gram* would print pictures on their front page of the young men from Oshkosh who were in the armed services. There were gold stars displayed in many windows throughout the city indicating a loved one was lost in the war. I remember reading some of the headlines about the Allies and Axis in the *Northwestern*. There would be maps in the paper with arrows showing how our troops were advancing. We would cheer for the Allies.

Although my life as a 3rd grader went on without worry or concern the people of Oshkosh did its share to support the war effort.

My dad was the air raid warden for our block. I believe every block had one. There would be times when the city would have a practice alert. The alarm would be sounded and my dad would circle the block with his government issued helmet and gas mask and make sure everyone had their lights out. This was serious business. If someone was smoking on their front porch during these blackouts, my dad had the authority to make the person put out his cigarette.

Gas was rationed. Everyone who drove a car would get stamps that allowed them to buy a limited amount of gas each month. If the car owner had a job that required travel, he could apply for additional stamps. There were also rationing stamps provided for meat, sugar, coffee, butter and a variety of other food items.

There was a nationwide effort to collect aluminum in support of the war. Oshkosh had a collection site on the corner of Algoma and Jackson in what was then Krambo Food Store's parking lot. It's now the site of the City Safety Building. There was a big circle of pans maybe 10 feet high. Many Oshkosh residents contributed their old cookware which then was melted down and reused for war materials.

Collection of scrap metal for the war effort

By the summer of 1945 the Allied forces were taking control. Germany had surrendered and we were closing in on Japan in the Pacific Theater. An atomic bomb was dropped August 6 on Hiroshima and another on Nagasaki three days later. Japan surrendered on August 15, 1945. The war was over.

That night our family, like most everyone else in town, went down to Main Street. The streets were crowded with people. Most everyone was yelling, dancing, laughing, lots of hugging and kissing. A band was playing, confetti was flying. It was the happiest time in many years. It was a sight that I will never forget.

For the first 10 years of my life, the world was at war with all its killing and suffering. But in my own neighborhood for a youngster still counting his age in single digits life was good.

Marcile Simm said she remembers where she was when the war started.

You remember moments like this. I was a teacher at South Park Junior High and was in the school library talking to Kathy Fitz, the librarian. President Roosevelt's voice came over the loudspeaker with an official Declaration of War. We were solemn and quiet and felt some chills. Kathy's fiancé was in the service.

Some rationing was the law of the land. We had rationing of sugar, butter, chocolate, coffee, meat and shoes. We each received an allotment of stamps from the government. I remember I had appendicitis during this time. One of my nurses told me she didn't know what she was going to do about shoes as her family already used up all their shoe stamps. I had my father go into our ration book to get a stamp which I gave to her to purchase shoes for work.

No amount of money could buy a pound of coffee unless you had the appropriate stamp. The price of a pound of coffee plus a ration stamp and you were really in business. We started saving foil and making it into balls, some 6 inches and some more than a foot. Junk lying around and worn out machine parts were saved as well as kitchen utensils. We once gave two iron frying pans to the government.

We started having blackout curtains a year or two into the war. There was a city representative who lived on our block. He would go around the block to see that no lights escaped from behind the curtains. This was done as an air raid precaution.

Eddy Gums and Donald Leonard, grocery store employees, enlisted in the Navy soon after the war started. When the two had leave they went back to their stores and passed out Hershey bars to friends and former customers. That was a treasure because you seldom saw a Hershey bar for sale during the war years.

Before the book was finished, I came in contact with a book entitled: *Last Wittnesses, An Oral History of the Children of World War II*. The author included memories of children who lived in the Minsk area in Russia when Germany invaded their country in World War II.

Included are two stories of children whose life and experiences in World War II, as you would expect, were much different than those of us who lived in Oshkosh.

Vera Novikova - Age 13

It was so long ago. . . But it's still frightening.

I remember such a sunny day. Our village is burning, our house is burning. We come out of the forest. The little children cry.

The house burned down. . . We rummaged in the ashes, but didn't find anything. Only charred forks. The stove stayed as it had stood. There was food in it – potato pancakes. Mama took the frying pay out with her hands. "Eat children." It was impossible to eat those pancakes, they smelled so much of smoke, but we ate them, because we had nothing else but grass. All we had left was the grass and the ground.

It was so long ago. . . But it's still frightening.

My cousin was hanged. . . Her husband was the commander of a partisan unit and she was pregnant. Someone denounced her to the Germans and they came. They chased everybody out to the square. Ordered that no one should cry. Next to the village council grew a tall tree. They drove the horse up to it.

They put the noose around her neck, she took the braid out of it. The horse pulled the sledge away and she hung their spinning.

The women shouted... They shouted without tears, just with voices. We weren't allowed to cry. We could shout but not cry – not be sorry. They came up and killed those who cried. There were adolescent boys, sixteen or seventeen years old. They were shot. They had cried.

Why have I told you this? It's more frightening for me now than then.

Lena Kraechenko – age seven

Of course I knew nothing about death... No one had time to explain it, but I just saw it.

When the machine guns rattle away from an airplane, it feels as it all the bullets are aimed at you. In your direction. I begged, "Mama dear, lie on me... She wouldn't lie on me and then I didn't see or hear anything.

Most frightening was to lose mama... I saw a dead young woman with a baby nursing at her breast. She must have been killed a minute before. The baby didn't even cry. And I was sitting right there.

As long as I don't lose mama... Mama holds my hand all the time and strokes my head. "Everything will be all right. Everything will be all right."

We rode in some truck. Then I remember we're being driven in a column. They're taking my mama away from me. I seize her hands, I clutch at her dress, she wasn't dressed for war. It was her fancy dress. Her best. I won't let go. I cry. The fascist shoves me aside first with his submachine gun and then when I'm on the ground with his boot. Some woman picks me up. Now she and I are for some reason riding on a train. Where? She calls me Anechka. But I think I had a different name. I seem to remember that it was different but what it was I forgot.

From fear. From fear that they'd taken my mama from me. Where are we going? I seem to understand from the conversation of the adults that we're being taken to Germany. I remember my thoughts. Why do the Germans need such a little girl? What am I going to do there? When it grew dark, the woman took me to the door of the car and just pushed me out" "Run for it! Maybe you'll save yourself."

I landed in some ditch and fell asleep there. It was cold and I dreamed that mama was wrapping me in something warm and saying gentle words. I've had that dream all my life.

Chapter Fifteen
The Corner Grocery

The corner grocery store was one of the neighborhood fixtures during those growing-up years in the 1940s and '50s, a place not often experienced anymore, where the grocer personally waited on each customer and you waited your turn.

There were sixteen of these small, mostly family-owned stores within five blocks of where I lived. None of them remain today. They simply could not compete with the prices, the selection and variety provided in larger food stores. So they went the way of the horse and buggy and black and white TV.

They were viewed as much as a social center by the customer as they were viewed as a business by the owner. There was a humanness there, a neighborliness that didn't exist in the larger stores. It was a place where you sat and visited with friends and with the owner when he wasn't tending to customers. It was a place to drink a pop, eat a candy bar, and, after your grocery list was filled, say to the owner, write it up.

The corner grocery store was an integral part of our community as were the church, the school and the neighborhood tavern. Each helped provide a sense of stability, a restraint, a sense of order and belonging most neighborhoods had years ago.

My mother did her weekly shopping on Fridays at Krogers, a south side supermarket, when their advertised specials competed favorably with Krambos and the A&P, both downtown stores. Even though the bought groceries would fill, sometimes spill over the kitchen table upon her return, the supply, with 6 boys and a husband to feed, would not last much beyond the weekend.

The fill-ins, the loaf of bread, the quart of milk, the pound of butter, the ring of bologna, items a family needed to carry them through to the next Friday were bought during the week at the corner grocery. And, if you had a sense of loyalty, you bought them at the one in your neighborhood.

In our neighborhood the store was Ploetzs.

Ploetz's Grocery

The owner of this store with a concrete step walkup was Fred Ploetz, who along with his wife Erma, his son Harry, and Harry's wife Florence and their two small children, Stevie and Joanie resided in the same building.

It was not the best of arrangements.

I was sometimes sent there by my mother to buy a loaf of bread, a pound of butter or some other stop-gap staple she felt would be safe to buy. But it was mostly a stopping-off place on my way home from school or from visiting a friend or when I was bored and could not think of anything else to do.

I was on a first-name basis with the Ploetzes. I often "shot the breeze" with Fred and the Mrs. but usually I would just sit, have a pop, watch and listen, waiting for the social dynamics of this extended family to kick in.

Mr. Ploetz was Fred to most everyone, even to us kids, who frequented the place. He didn't seem to mind. He was, I suppose, in his sixties during my growing-up years, although to a youngster in his teens and pre-teens, old was old. He was an easy-going conversationalist and a bit of a philosopher when the mood struck, but was also quiet and introspective when the strain of running the store became too much.

Mrs. Ploetz (she was the Mrs. to me as she was to her husband as in "The Mrs. Is on a rampage again") was a veritable dynamo. She packed into her small frame a force of energy that in its directness knew no bounds. When she was angry she was unrelenting in her verbalness as if on a mission to exact the full price of the wrath she so often carried. She could be soft and caring too, but not when she carried the banner" "Protector of the Brood."

The weakness of the mother was spoiling.

Harry was the only child of Fred and Erma and despite his age and having a wife and family, he remained stuck in the early stages of adolescence. He was not allowed to grow up, to take on responsibility, to fail. And he was not held accountable for his actions.

The Mrs. Still coddled Harry at the age of 35.

Harry, who could usually be seen in-and-around the store when he wasn't drinking, had a bad work history. He had a hard time holding down a steady job due to his drinking and his inability to take orders. His lack of independence and lack of a steady income was the source of many arguments between father and son.

It was not always an idyllic place to be.

The relationship revealed itself in ways familiar to fathers and sons who become alienated. But in one way, clearly apparent to anyone who made a purchase in the store, it took on an unconventional even bizarre form of conduct although those unaware of the social dynamics of the place, a connection between father and his aberrant son may not have been made.

It was Fred's new system of money management.

His garb – a pair of pants and a vest with four pockets – was his modus operandi. He kept quarters in one vest pocket, half dollars in another, and dimes and nickels in the remaining two. The folding money –dollars and five dollar bills – were kept in his two front pants pockets. The big money he placed in his wallet and his wallet usually bulged.

The pennies were left in the cash register.

He did this because his son, when in need of money, would simply help himself to the contents of the cash register and use it to go on a toot. With this easy access to his drinking money was stopped, Harry's temper fed on his need for escape. And at those times his rage would quickly and predictably be picked up his mother's antenna.

Whatever the Mrs. was doing it was quickly put down.

I can still see her coming from the back room, housedress and apron on, rayon stockings rolled halfway to her knees, slippers too big for her feet, walking her walk – it was actually a fast shuffle as she tilted from side to side – until she was right over Fred who was usually sitting in his black leather-like rocking chair at the rear of the store.

With her finger rocking back and forth as she pointed, she would scold Fred about his tightness, his lack of trust in his son, his unwillingness to let Harry assume more responsibility in the store's operation.

Her bombasity was unrelenting. She was loud and she was persistent. He didn't stand a chance.

Fred usually stayed and took it.

He wanted to escape the anger of his wife but also wanted to be in the store for his customers. The intricacy of the situation was his fear that Harry might keep the money if he was not there, and even if that didn't matter, unless the customers had the exact change Harry could not make the transaction.

Sometimes it seemed that nothing mattered. The incessant nagging and the temper outburst would take their toll and Fred had to get away.

But the choices of escape were limited to this store owner past his prime. Sitting by his garage or walking in his garden were the usual choices. But the lot was small and distancing thin and if the anguish was deep enough I might see him walk across the street to the corner tavern to hoist a few. At least he had someone to talk to in there, someone who might lend an understanding ear, someone who would nod in agreement to his complaints about "this whole damned situation."

If all this was not enough, the rest of the family treated the store as their own pantry. They seemed to take what they wanted without regard to hygiene and good business practice. Fred sometimes put his foot down but usually backed off realizing that the strain of arguing and getting upset was too high a price to pay. It was easier to sit in his old black easy chair reading, snoozing, often just staring off in the distance.

His thoughts were his own.

Nothing seemed to bother him then. Maybe it was his way of shutting out the outside world. Even when Joanie and Stevie were running between the kitchen and the stairway leading to the upstairs and the Mrs. hollering, oftentimes cussing, frequently in German, for the kids to come back and finish their suppers, Fred remained composed.

It all seemed so strange.

Mother was reluctant to shop at Ploetzes. She knew too many people were handling the food and too few people were shopping there. "Make sure it's fresh" were often her parting words as I headed off across the street. And when she needed sandwich meat for packing lunches, she put me on notice that Mr. Ploetz was to use the meat cutter and not his knives to cut slices from his loaves of meat.

"He cuts too thick."

And the store was dirty. Most every can or box of food sold, when taken from the top shelf, was thick with dust. Fred would sometimes blow the dust of the top of the container before wiping it with a cloth hung nearby. If the cloth could not be found his sleeve would do. "That won't hurt a thing," he liked to say.

My mother simply would not go in the store. We bought a few things there only because of Dad's insistence. Loyalty was important to him.

"You're a good boy Ronnie," the Mrs. would sometimes say when her thoughts were on a few of the older kids who helped themselves when they thought the Ploetzes were not looking. It made me feel good when they took me in like this.

Later on I realized that, like most families living under strain, the Ploetzes went about their business and stayed in their own world as much as they could. They made their way and lived their lives as many of us do today. But to a young, impressionable boy, this family, this place on the corner, unlike all of the others, left its mark.

I still think of Fred and Mrs. and Harry and the kids. I think of the store and the dust and dirt, the voices in the back, and the smell of supper on the stove. I think of Fred's hand-driven meat cutter and sharp knives, his empty cash register and pockets full of money. I think of his bulk cookie display, his five cent grab bags, his magnifying glass and his clock repair station. And I think of the few regular customers who shopped there out of neighborhood loyalty, and of Dad who became a friend of the Ploetzes; all of them.

Above all else, when my mind turns to the corner of 12th and Minnesota is a place where I could go, drink a pop, eat a candy bar and sometimes "chew the fat" with Fred and the Mrs. or just sit and while away time before heading off across the street.

Chapter Sixteen
EWECO Park

At different times and with different owners, it featured a roller coaster, vaudeville acts, a theater, dance pavilion, roller skating rink, swimming beach, bathhouse, baseball diamond with a covered grandstand, a Ferris Wheel and Merry-Go-Round, two bandstands, two concession booths, an outdoor movie theater, a water toboggan chute, and a host of other attractions that for a short time included performances by aerialists, high wire walkers and acrobats that brought thousands to this place along the shores of Lake Winnebago three miles south of Oshkosh. It was called the Coney Island of Oshkosh and was once the largest entertainment attraction in the city.

It opened on Sunday, June 19, 1898 as an Electric Park. The *Northwestern,* the following day, wrote that "there was a pushing, scrambling crowd eager to get to it. The place resembled a miniature Coney Island."

Nine months earlier the city converted their horse-drawn streetcars with streetcars powered by electricity. Tracks were laid that ended at the city limits. To increase revenues, companies frequently bought land at the end of the line and created recreational parks to draw people on the weekend.

The city's Citizens' Traction Company, thinking along those same lines, purchased 20 acres of land in March of 1898 for the purpose of creating their own Electric Park.

William Waters, the prominent Oshkosh architect, was hired to design the park's buildings. A two story dance pavilion, a summer theater, two band stands, a bathhouse and two refreshment booths were soon built.

EWECO Park

The Citizen's Traction Company, anxious to bring Oshkosh residents to the new park on weekends, extended the electric street car route to the entrance of the park. Best of all the fare from any point in the city to the park was only 5 cents. This was exciting news for the city's residents who were then facing the beginnings of both the Spanish-American War and the Oshkosh Woodworker's Strike.

The interurban rail lines connecting the cities of Appleton, Neenah, Menasha, Fond du Lac, Oshkosh and Omro were being built about the same time. This new transit system also brought many adult residents from neighboring communities to enjoy what the new park offered.

Much of the early advertisement featured the park as a place to relax and cool off. The shady trees, garden swings and cool breezes off the lake were welcome means of relief from the summer heat. For 15 cents swimmers, both men and women, could rent a towel, a bathing suit and a locker and then enjoy wading out two hundred feet on a sandy lake bottom. Swimming in public was a new idea especially for women.

Eight years later the park was sold and renamed White City.

Plans were made to rebuild the park to resemble the famous White City amusement park in Chicago. Changes were made to attract more customers. The spectacle of lights and the repainting of the buildings in white along with a roller coaster, an outdoor motion picture theater and a lighted fountain attracted many more to the park located three miles south of town.

Electric Street Car on Main Street

A few years later, due to financial difficulties, the park was once again transformed to a place where families gathered to enjoy swimming, roller skating and to experience a quiet time in the park.

By 1917 the popularity of the park had declined as it was now possible to dance at a number of places in Oshkosh and movie theaters offered three different features a week. But the streetcar company, under yet another name: Eastern Wisconsin Electric Company was determined to revive the park.

A contest was held to rename the rejuvenated the park. Adolf Menzel won the contest by using the initials of the name of the company that owned the park, and named it EWECO Park.

In October of 1925 streetcars ran to EWECO for the last time and buses took over the line. It was sold again ten years later to Charles Maloney, an experienced dance promoter who also owned the Cinderella Ballroom in Appleton. Couples paid 60 cents to dance in the park's dance pavilion to the music of nationally renowned bands that often made the circuit in central Wisconsin.

Rita Malchow, the daughter of Charles Maloney, heard from one of her friends - someone I knew - that I was doing a story on the park, called and invited me to her apartment on Wisconsin Avenue for an interview.

This is her story.

"My dad sold the park in April of 1954. The driveway for the park was directly across the road from a gas station or mini-mart that is no longer there. I recall there was a motel right in back."

"Our driveway was between the Stanley Hall residence to the north and the road leading into Paukotuk to the south. The road went straight in and Dad owned the whole section that extended to the lake. Dad eventually bought Dr. Conley's Paukotuk house but that wasn't included as part of the park property."

"There were eight in our family and most of us were still young during those early years. We were allowed to go down to the dance hall for fifteen to twenty minutes to watch on a night when a big band was playing. They didn't allow us to dance however. Some of the bands I remember were Guy Lombardo, Kay Keyser, Eddie Howard, Lawrence Welk,

Tommy and Jimmy Dorsey and Ted Weems. Sunday entertainment, I remember, featured local bands."

The big dance bands when making the circuit in this part of Wisconsin would appear at most of the popular dance halls in the area including the Cinderella, the Raveno in Neenah, Waverly Beach in Menasha and EWECO Park in Oshkosh. Ballroom dancing was big in the 1930s and '40s during the Big Band era.

"Dad was in the dance hall business. That's why he bought EWECO Park. He owned the Cinderella Ballroom in Appleton and also ran roller skating rinks at different locations in Oshkosh. He also owned the Playmore, a dance hall upstairs in the first block of South Main Street beyond the bridge. I remember going there with my parents to watch parades passing by."

"My dad owned the Waverly Beach property. We had a home there too. At that time Waverly was just a dance hall. Later on it included a bar and restaurant and an outdoor patio for entertainment. I was there a couple of years ago for a Friday night fish fry and didn't recognize the place. It changed so much that it was difficult to picture what it looked like when my dad owned it. I remember there was a huge sign out front that read: 'Waverly Beach Ballroom.'"

"My dad built the Cinderella Ballroom. On Sundays Dad ran the bands at the Cinderella and my mother ran the bands at EWECO Park."

"I remember Eddie Howard coming to our EWECO Park cottage. He and Dad would sit around the table talking and signing contracts. There were other band leaders who did the same. But I do remember Eddie Howard being there. I didn't pay much attention to the business at hand as I was still very young."

"We always had a big party on the 4th. My dad's birthday

was July 6 and we always celebrated two days early. Family, relatives and many friends would attend. Dad would put up some of the out-of-town guests in the Conley house."

I asked why her dad bought the Conley property other than to put up guests one time during the year.

"My dad bought property, that's what he did. I think he also may have bought it to keep out intruders and to have a place to put up guests. The property was in Paukotuk adjacent to the park. It was a lovely place on the lake. The Conley's, for some reason, never lived there."

"The park was a very popular place. That I do remember. The dancehall always seemed to be packed. If my older siblings were still alive they could tell you so much more. I was just not that interested in the park during my early years."

Soon after, I received a call from Ken Widmer. Ken and his wife Jean lived on East Elm Street in Chandlish Harbor. The two farmed on Country Club Road for years until they built their Chandlish Harbor house in 1966 in what was once known as EWECO Park.

"So much of the original park was gone when we went to the park to dance. It was just a dancehall then. Beer and pop was sold but no hard liquor."

Jean said there were no flush toilets in the building. "They were 'outdoor toilets' inside. At times the air quality near the lavatory was not the best."

They said that every Sunday night while they were dating the two went out to EWECO Park in the summer to dance. In the winter they danced at the Eagles. The two, like so many of the time, loved to dance.

"Frank Chandlish bought the place from Charlie Maloney to get rid of what he called the 'Den of Inequity.' The property had been owned by Frank's father before Maloney bought it and his son wanted it back."

"When the sale was finalized, the first thing he did was to have the dancehall torn down. "I'm going to have the area sodded and then sell lots for residential homes.' He was determined that the Weyerhorst Creek be turned into Chandlish Harbor. Frank had the creek dredged and used the soil to fill the lots."

Following the interview, Ken and I drove around the development on a road that paralleled the creek that was dredged and widened. While he was telling me who once occupied some of these beautiful homes, I was trying to envision this place as it once was; a recreation mecca once known as Oshkosh's Coney Island with its roller coaster, its water toboggan, its two bandstands, and a host of other attractions that drew people throughout this part of the Midwest.

What a time that must have been.

Chapter Seventeen
Oshkosh All Stars

Its beginning happened in 1929 when Arthur Heywood, an *Oshkosh Northwestern* sports editor, proposed in his sport's column that Oshkosh should have a professional basketball team. It was needed for the citizenry, he argued, to have something to do and talk about during those long winter months.

The idea was soon picked up by Lonnie Darling, an Oshkosh seed distributer and salesman for the G.H. Hunkel Company, who, despite never having played a game in his life, soon began recruiting local players for the team.

They began as an amateur barnstorming team playing against teams in Wisconsin and as far away as Chicago and Detroit. The team had no set roster and players made anywhere from $15 to $25 per game, which, if not top money then, was far better than many other job opportunities offered.

They started playing basketball at the Recreation Gym on Division Street and later, after they joined the National Basketball League, played their home games at Merrill Junior High and then at South Park Junior High when the school was built in 1940.

The Sport played an important part in our city's history as you will discover when reading the following four sport stories including this one of the Oshkosh All Stars.

It was an era when professional basketball was still played in small cities, when the landscape was dotted with franchises across the Midwest, and a period when Oshkosh was known for something other than bib overalls, wood chips, and Saturday night brawls on Main Street. It was the time of our own Oshkosh All Stars and the National Basketball League. Rules of the game were different from today's game, and the antiquated rules made it impossible for high-scoring contests. After every basket, the ball went back to mid-court for a center jump while the clock continued non-stop. That part of the game would change a few years later.

The All Stars played during a time when two-hand set shots and one hand push shots and underhand free throw shooting was the fashion of the day; when the tallest player might be six foot five or six and a good night might bring 10 points across from your name.

The All Stars continued to play games in Oshkosh and in a variety of other places in Wisconsin and in neighboring states and were considered a success during those years as an amateur team. In the mid-1930s they discarded their amateur status and became an unaffiliated professional team. Their goal was to join the National Basketball League being formed in the Midwest.

To help this effort the All Stars decided to become the first team to be involved in an interracial professional basketball game and what may have been one of the first interracial sporting events in American history. The all-white Oshkosh team would compete against an all-black team from New York. The New York team was the New York Renaissance, known as the Rens.

It was considered by many, in and outside of basketball circles, as a dangerous and unseemly marketing venture by each of the teams. Interracial mixing was offensive and repulsive to many whites at the time and was prohibited in many of the states.

But the two games drew such large crowds that they decided

to continue the series. The large turnouts were not lost on Lonnie Darling or Robert Douglas, owner of the Rens. Because of its success the two owners decided to play a five game series that were scheduled in Oshkosh, Racine, Green Bay, Ripon and Madison, places where the interracial games could be played.

The Oshkosh team lost to the Rens 3 games to 2. But because of the continued popularity of the games the two owners decided that it would be in the interest of both teams to extend the series again by playing two more games.

Ever the shrewd promoter, Darling declared that by extending the series to seven games it should be considered as the "World Series" of basketball. If the All Stars would win these two games they would be, at least in Darling's mind, the new world's basketball champions. They won and in 1936 the National Basketball League (NBL) added Oshkosh as a founding member.

Within two years the *Chicago Herald American*, aware of the fan interest in the games between the Rens and the All Stars and the publicity it produced, started a giant event called the World Championship of Professional Basketball. They invited the top 12 professional teams in the country. The winner would become the undisputed world champion of professional basketball.

Kareem Abdul Jabbar in his book: *On The Shoulders of Giants* wrote about that first world championship tournament.

"On March 28, 1939 eight young black men from Harlem anxiously stood on the polished wooden floor of the Chicago Coliseum facing nine white men in the championship game of the first ever World Professional Basketball Tournament. Surrounding them was a sold-out crowd of three thousand raucous fans – most of them white, most of them shouting out the name of their favorites – the Oshkosh All Stars."

Oshkosh residents waiting to greet and honor the arrival of the National Basketball Champion Oshkosh All Stars.

The organizers of the tournament invited what they considered as the top twelve teams in basketball. Two of the teams invited were black: the Rens and the Harlem Globetrotters. This was the first time white and black teams faced each other for the world title.

The All Stars lost to the New York Rens that year in the championship game 34 to 25. Three years later in 1942, 4,000 All Star fans waited at the railroad depot on Broad Street to greet their world Champion Oshkosh All Stars.

Leroy "Lefty" Edwards was the premier player on the All Stars since joining fulltime in 1937 just as the National Basketball League was being formed. He quickly made a name for himself on the pro circuit and became a dominant player and a gate attraction.

During his career Edwards was named All League First Team 6 times and was twice named to the All-League Second Team. He was there at the beginning of the NBL and there at the end.

In 1945, near the end of this pro career, Edwards was named to the All-Time Professional Basketball Team. The article in the *Northwestern* commemorating the selection reads in part: "Three members of the original New York Celtics and two present-day players were named as basketball's all-time professional team today by the six coaches and managers of the National Basketball League."

"Bobby McDermott, Fort Wayne Zollner Pistons, Leroy (Cowboy) Edwards, Oshkosh All Stars, and Nat Homan, Harry (Dutch) Dehnert and John Beckman, all of the old Celtic team were nominated as the game's greatest professional players in a poll conducted by *United Press*."

Edwards, known as Lefty or Cowboy started playing in Oshkosh in 1935 when the All Stars were still an amateur team. Edwards was voted into the Basketball Hall of Fame in 1971 and was one of two Oshkosh players – the other being Charlie Shipp – on the NBL's all-time team. Besides his scoring average and his patented left-hand hook shots, Lefty had a reputation for his "defensive skills."

Sandy Padive in his book, *Basketball's Hall of Fame*, writes about George Mikan, who he called the first of the great big men.

"In 1946, George Mikan signed with the Chicago Gears of the NBL. The Gears were playing the team from Oshkosh, Wisconsin and the Wisconsin team had a center named Cowboy Edwards who introduced this up-and-coming basketball star by knocking out four of Mikan's teeth."

There were exhibitions played before the start of the regular season and a few were squeezed in during league play. The opponents included the annual appearance of the bearded Michigan House of David and a few colored teams as they were then called.

The Chicago Collegians, a barnstorming colored team,

occasionally started off the exhibition season. Nate Clifton and the New York Rens, recognized as the premier professional basketball team of the 1930s, would play here now and then as would the Globetrotters.

The All Stars didn't seem to draw well when they came to play. Maybe it was the strangeness of it all, a feeling of discomfort in a city where blackness was confined to its tarred roadways. For some it may have been the perceived inferior play of those who were relegated as second-class citizens even in the sports world.

The late war years were a difficult time for the All Stars. In 1945 they missed the league playoffs for the only time in their history.

The 1946-47 season was expected to be a successful year for the team. Gene Englund and Bob Carpenter were back from the war and the 6 foot, 6 inch Clint Wager was back with the team. Lefty Edwards, logging 10 years with the team, was still a very good player. Jack Maddox, a guard from Texas, was also added.

In a meeting of the Lions Club held at the Hotel Athearn in September of 1946, Lonnie Darling stated that a larger gymnasium with a seating capacity of 5,000 would be highly desirable for the community and for the All Stars. He went on to say that the All Stars played in the smallest home gym and have the lowest salary schedule in each of the two professional basketball leagues: the NBL and the BAA (Basketball Association of America), a league that played on the east coast.

A few days later at a noon meeting with the Rotary Club at the Athearn, Darling continued with his message. He stated that the All Stars carried the name of Oshkosh throughout the country in a way that is scarcely appreciated by the greater number of residents of the city. "It is the only time Oshkosh teams have been represented in a major league of any kind, and the All Stars symbolize Oshkosh in the minds of millions of people."

Despite the urgency of the matter an arena was not built.

Although the All Stars did not win the Western Conference that year, they did have an outstanding season. They came in second behind the powerful Indianapolis Kautskys, but did compete against the Fort Wayne Zollner Pistons in the finals of the World Championship Tournament in Chicago. The All Stars were hoping they could repeat as world champions but the Pistons had other plans. They beat the All Stars and won the title for the third consecutive year.

In 1948, the NBL began merging with the BAA forming the National Basketball Association, the NBA. Despite a few NBL teams merging with the newly formed NBA, most notably the Minneapolis Lakers and the Fort Wayne Zollner Pistons, the NBL continued for one more year.

In 1948-49, the leagues last, the All Stars won the Western Division playoff against the Tri-Cities Blackhawks and their seven foot center Don Otten, a time when seven foot centers were a rarity. They lost the NBL championship to the Anderson Packers in three straight games.

A few additional NBL teams were invited to join the NBA that year including the Syracuse Nationals, Rochester Royals and the Tri-Cities Blackhawks. Even the Sheboygan Redskins were invited. Oshkosh was not.

Its undoing was unavoidable. Salaries began to soar and the All Stars couldn't keep up with the player's demands. South Park could hold only 2,100 fans. The money needed to support the team just couldn't be raised, ending a relatively short but certainly memorable era in Oshkosh sport's history.

It was disappointing for many of us who watched the All

Stars and listened to them on the radio. No longer would the Rookie of the Year, Dolph Schayes of the Nationals or the scoring tandem of George Mikan and Jim Pollard of the Lakers ply their trade in a gymnasium a few blocks removed from the center of our universe. Bob Davie, Al Cervi and Red Holtzman of the Royals, Bobby McDermott of the Pistons, Frank Brian of the Anderson Packers, Mel Riebe of the Cleveland Transfers and Eddie Dancker of the Redskins would also be among those missing. They would now compete in the league that featured "Jumping' Joe Fuchs of the Philadelphia Warriors and "Easy" Ed McCauley of the Boston Celtics.

Tom Hansen recalls what many of us remember about those days.

The last gym the All Stars played in was South Park Junior High. Many of us who attended that school in the late 1940s occasionally saw the All Stars walking in the school corridors during our class time and when we passed the gymnasium during class changes we usually stopped to peak in during their practices. And when the All Stars played their league games, my friends and I were regular fans in the west bleachers on stage. Believe it or not, the admission was 25 cents for kids to get in.

It is interesting to note that the All-Time NBL scoring leaders from 1937-1949 included two All Stars in the top three. Leroy Edwards followed Bobby McDermott at number two, and Gene Englund was number three. Down the list in eighth place was Bob Carpenter, another All Star.

Lonnie Darling was the heart and soul of the All Stars. He coached, signed and paid the players and ran the club until it folded in 1949. He had a hard time coping with the loss of the All Stars. It was his life for the past twenty years. He died two years later in 1951 of a heart attack. He was 48.

It should be noted that the National Basketball League was the first professional basketball league to integrate, helping to break down racial barriers in sports. During the 1942-43 season ten African-American players played in Toledo and Chicago because many former players were serving in the armed forces.

The NBA, the professional basketball league of today, finally integrated in 1950 adding three African-American players: Earl Lloyd with the Washington Capitols, Chuck Cooper with the Boston Celtics and Nat "Sweetwater" Clifton with the New York Knicks. A few years later professional basketball games would radically change when team rosters included future Hall of Famers, Elgin Baylor, Oscar Robertson, Wilt Chamberlain and Bill Russell.

A few of the All Stars would sign and play for the Oshkosh Stars, a semi-pro team organized the following year in the newly formed Wisconsin State Basketball League.

But it soon became painfully clear that the Oshkosh Stars led by local favorites Charlie and Eddie Erban and former All Stars, Bill McDonald, Gene Berce, Billy Reed and Bob Mulvihill with occasional help from an old and tired Edwards and a semi-retired Englund would never replace Lonnie Darlings' World Champion Oshkosh All Stars, a team led by a left-hand hook shot artist, Hall of Fame coach Adolph Rupp of Kentucky would later call the greatest player he ever coached.

Chapter Eighteen
Baseball

*B**aseball occupied a good part of American sports entertainment in the days before and after the Civil War. Baseball clubs were organized in most every city and rural towns in the land and the most intense rivalries were with neighboring communities.*

The city of Oshkosh, like so many other communities throughout the country, has its own baseball story.

Oshkosh fielded its first team in 1865, just 12 years after receiving the city charter. The team was known as the Everetts. They played against other amateur clubs from neighboring cities. Home games were played on a field with fenced-in bleachers on the south side of New York Avenue between Jackson and Main streets.

Another amateur team was formed called the "Amateurs" and they played teams in and around the state until 1886 when Oshkosh's first professional baseball team was organized. The Oshkosh team joined what was then known as the Northwestern League. They played their home games at the old fairgrounds at Murdock and Jackson.

The Oshkosh entry would later be remembered by fielding a player by the name of William "Dummy" Hoy from Ohio. Hoy would play fourteen years in the Major Leagues.

As fate would have it, Hoy was unable to hear the cheers from the fans in the grandstand. Hoy, who was deaf, thus the name "Dummy," was instrumental in getting umpires to change from voice to hand signals when calling plays.

The league was forced to fold because of an economic

depression that spread throughout the country during the decades of the 1880s.

At the turn of the century Oshkosh joined with other cities of its size in the Wisconsin-Illinois League. The Indians, as they were then called, won league titles in 1912, 1913 and '14 and had three future major league baseball players on their roster; Heinie Groh, Hall of Fame pitcher Addie Joss, and Oshkosh resident Albert "Cozy" Dolan.

The Indians folded in 1914 due to the war in Europe and professional baseball wouldn't return in our city for another 27 years, other than a much-watched exhibition game between two major league baseball clubs.

In August of 1934, a baseball event, mostly forgotten in this city, was an exhibition game played at the old County Fairgrounds on Murdock Street between the Chicago Cubs and the St. Louis Cardinals.

The exhibition game was arranged by Frank Steckbauer, according to Harry Hurst, the author of the book "Random thoughts of Nordheim." Steckbauer was the manager of the downtown Continental Clothing Store. He was a civic leader as well as an avid baseball fan. And he knew Bob Lewis, the Cub's traveling secretary, who, it was said, had an Oshkosh connection.

"They played in the old fairgrounds where the baseball diamond was right in front of the grandstand. To accommodate the many fans they expected for the game, they brought bleachers in from as far away as Appleton and Fond du Lac to line the baselines and the outfield. They had an overflow crowd of 12,000 paid admissions."

According to the same source, the two teams arrived at the Chicago Northwestern Depot on Broad Street at 12:30 P.M. on the day of the game. Each team had its own railroad coach plus a dining car to share. They were greeted by large crowds at the depot, at their hotels, as well as at the gate of the fairgrounds. The Cubs went to the Athearn Hotel where a reception was held for them. The Cards went to the Raulf Hotel where they refused a reception and went right up to change into their uniforms. They arrived at the fairgrounds in a fleet of cabs and signed autographs on the way in.

"Many celebrities were on hand including Governor Schmedeman, U.S. Senator Ryan Duffy, Congressman Michael Reilly and many more. Mayor Oaks declared a half-holiday so the working people could see the game. "Beans" Reardon was the umpire behind the plate and Bill Klem, the National League's chief umpire, was on first base. They had a local favorite, "Opie" Below on third base. Dizzy" Dean, the Cards ace pitcher, was the public address announcer. He kept the crowd entertained with his hillbilly humor. He also told the fans that they were looking at the next World Champions."

Major League Baseball Game at the County Fairgrounds

"The Cards were managed by Frankie Frisch and he used Jim Mooney and Dazzy Vance as pitchers that day. There were many long hits in the game. Because of the overflow crowd in the outfield, anything in the crowd was only a two-base hit as fans were sitting on the grass in front of all the bleachers. If the game was of any significance, it was the fact that ten of those players on the two teams are enshrined in the Baseball Hall of Fame in Cooperstown. But most of the fans were just glad to see their old Cub favorites: Gabby Hartnett, Kiki Cuyler, Charley Grimm, Lon Warnecke, Charlie Root, Guy Bush and Woody English."

In 1940 the Wisconsin State League was formed. Oshkosh was not included the first year due to numerous obstacles that needed to be overcome including not having an adequate playing field. Sawyer Avenue Ballpark (it's now the home of the Zion Lutheran Church) was soon built and the Oshkosh team was ready to play ball on opening day in May of 1941.

Sawyer Avenue Baseball Park. It is now the home of the Zion Lutheran Church

Oshkosh became a Boston Brave's farm club that year and was known as the Oshkosh Braves. Hank Bauer, who later played for the Casey Stengel's New York Yankee championship years in the 1940s and '50s played for the Oshkosh team that year. Also playing was Vernon "Swede" Erickson, the grandfather of Matt Erickson who is currently one of the batting instructors for the Milwaukee Brewers.

The following year the team was picked up by the New York Giants and renamed the Oshkosh Giants. The league discontinued during the war years of 1943, '44 and '45 but resumed operation in 1946. The league continued its operation for the next 8 years until the Boston Braves moved to Milwaukee when interest in minor league ball in and around the Milwaukee area was waning. The league disbanded in 1954.

Bill O'Donnell, who pitched for the Giants during their last year and married one of my high school classmates, and I became friends over the years, mostly of the long-distant variety. He knew I was writing another book and thought an interview with Dave Garcia, the most popular and venerated ballplayer and manager of the Giants, would be an important addition to the book. He called his former manager and set me up with his phone number.

Although I never thought it would come to pass, I dialed Garcia's number and after introducing myself, I mentioned that he was still remembered with great affection in Oshkosh.

"Some of the happiest moments in my life were in Oshkosh," was his opening line in our conversation, a conversation that lasted one hour and ten minutes owned almost entirely by Garcia's remembrances. I mostly sat back and listened.

Dave grew up in East St. Louis as a youngster and was a member of the St. Louis Cardinal and St. Louis Brown's knothole gang. Those kids were admitted free of charge to many of the Cardinal and Brown's games, and Dave grew up idolizing "Ducky" Medwick and "Pepper" Martin of the

"Gashouse Gang."

He grew up with the Bauers,' Herman and Hank. Both Dave and Hank were invited to spring training in 1941 with a team from Grand Forks, North Dakota. It was 13 degrees when they reported. Dave was eventually offered a $100 a month contract from the club and Hank was sent to Oshkosh where he signed for $75 a month. The Oshkosh ball club was a farm club of the Boston Braves at the time and was known as the Oshkosh Braves. Later Hank Bauer played for the New York Yankees during their championship years of the 1950s.

When I asked Dave about his memories of Oshkosh, he cited close friendships with Ollie Davis, owner of the City Cab and the Terminal Restaurant, and with Harold Schumurth, football coach of Oshkosh High. He also mentioned friendships with John Nevers, Killian Spanbauer, Ralph Mosling, "Swede" Erickson, Bill MacDonald, Gene Englund of the All Stars and Bob Kolf, football coach at the college.

Dave and his wife Carmen lived in Oshkosh from 1949 to 1961, eight years after the Giant franchise folded. He and his family of two girls and one boy lived in a house on 20th and Doty near the south side bathing beach. He said it was the best house he ever lived in.

The Winnebago Baseball League is a reminder of an earlier time when amateur baseball was played on Sunday afternoons. Driving to the ball diamond and cheering for their hometown team was a Sunday ritual as clear as watching and rooting for the Green Bay Packers is today.

I met with John Lenz, the league's president and Ken and Joan Koplitz to talk about the league that played in hamlets and small-road towns in the western part of Winnebago County.

"We played Sunday afternoons," John said. "None of the league diamonds had bleachers so spectators stood, brought lawn chairs or watched the game parked in their cars. Despite the lack of seating, we usually had a good crowd at every ballgame."

It was considered a social outing for area farmers, so they looked forward to game day. There were always pre-game stories in the *Northwestern,* a schedule for the day so area baseball enthusiasts and families, who wanted a Sunday afternoon outing could follow their team.

"The Hi-K Supper Club, located in Zion, was always busy after home games for players and families, and once in a while players would head over to EWECO Park after the game to check out the girls, dance a little and down a few beers."

It started in the summer of 1945 when teams from Winneconne, Omro, Poygan, Zion, Waukau, Eureka, Allenville and Readfield rounded out the league. Berlin, Neenah, Greenville, Dale and Oshkosh would at different times join later.

Orv Wonzer in his Time Out column in the *Oshkosh Northwestern* in the summer of 1962 wrote: "Don't think for a single moment that baseball isn't the national pastime. . . While nearly 50,000 jammed their way into Comiskey Park Sunday afternoon to watch the Chicago White Sox and the New York Yankees in the hot American League race, another gathering, much less in number but a million times more enthusiastic, jammed into all available space around the Poygan diamond to watch the Omro and Poygan teams clash in the championship game. It was reported that Sunday's crowd numbered more than one thousand and that it was the biggest crowd in Poygan history."

John Lenz said it all ended in the late '50s as the local talent got older and left and the attendance at the games went down. "We had huge crowds those first years. Crowds of one thousand were not rare. This was a way of life back then for area farmers and their families."

When the local players left the game, "outside players" were recruited. And when the locals saw fewer area players on their team attendance went down.

But there were other forces at work. Major League games were now being televised on Sunday afternoons, and in 1953 when the Boston Braves moved to Milwaukee, the team attracted people from all over the state including those games played on Sunday afternoons.

In the 1950s, Oshkosh High School had four baseball players that eventually made the major leagues. In all likelihood it may have been five had not Harry Gauger, considered one of the best to ever pitch for the high school, died in an auto accident after signing with the Detroit Tigers.

Billy Hoeft, a graduate of Oshkosh High in 1950 and one of the most sought after high school players in the history of the sport was one of the most sought-after players in the country.

This lanky port-sider, this 17 year old who was being watched by scouts from most major league clubs since his sophomore year, made baseball history by fanning 27 straight batters in the first game of the season in his senior year. TWENTY-SEVEN IN A ROW. Not one batter for the opposing team hit a fair ball. According to the scorer, no more than ten to twelve balls were fouled off.

Just how good was this left hander from the east side who amassed a record of 34 straight wins until losing one in the state tournament in his junior year. Jimmie Hole, a scout for Oakland of the Pacific Coast League, said that Hoeft was the best he ever saw.

After graduating from Oshkosh High in 1950, Hoeft declined several substantial bonus offers to sign with the Detroit Tigers. Unlike today when high school players sign for bonuses in the millions, the baseball rules of the time stated that if a player signed for a bonus of more than $6,000, the player must move up to the parent club after just one year of minor league seasoning.

After two years in the minor leagues, Hoeft made his first appearance in April of 1952 at the age of 19. The following year he secured a place in the Tiger's starting rotation where he remained until 1958.

In 1955 he recorded 16 wins and posted a 2.99 ERA while leading the league in shutouts with earning a spot on the American League All Star team. The following year he won 20 games.

His career ended in 1966 after playing for the Boston Red Sox, Baltimore Orioles, San Francisco Giants and the Milwaukee Braves. His major league record with 97 wins and 101 losses.

But if Hoeft was the best of the Oshkosh pitchers, Howie Koplitz was not far behind. As a sophomore he combined with senior Harry Gauger to pitch a no-hitter in the 1954 State Championship game. He pitched a perfect seven inning game with 21 strikeouts in 1956 and pitched a 10 – 0 two hit shutout with 16 strikeouts in the 1956 state Championship game. His record of striking out 114 and allowing only 15 hits in 52 innings while batting .533 with 7 homeruns and 25 RBIs during the '56 season, and his 15 and 1 high school pitching record, helps to complete the picture. Major League scouts, aware of the accomplishments of Gauger, Dave Tyriver and Koplitz soon flocked in droves to Oshkosh hoping to find another Hoeft.

Howie Koplitz, after considering a number of offers from major league clubs, chose to sign with the Detroit Tigers as did Hoeft six years before.

His professional career peaked in 1961 in Birmingham,

Alabama. It was about as close as one could come to a perfect year. He told me everything he tried worked. "I got in the groove early and stayed there."

He was named Minor Player of the Year and invited to the Topps Baseball Banquet at the Waldorf Astoria in New York City. On January 3, 1962 the *Sporting News* ran his picture on the front page along with Ralph Houk, Roger Maris and Warren Spahn."

When he returned to Detroit after a callup during the final month of the season, the Tigers and the Yankees were involved in a pennant race. Detroit lost out despite winning 103 games. During that pennant drive, Howie won 2 games without a loss for the Tigers.

"I wish I had the words to describe how I felt the first time I walked out on the field of Yankee Stadium. The same could be said for Fenway Park, Briggs Stadium and a host of others. There was a day in 1962 when Billy Hoeft, Dave Tyriver and I each pitched in a major league game. Not a bad testimony for 'Little Oshkosh.'"

In December of 1963, after a series of setbacks, the Washington Senators claimed him under Rule 5 when his options for staying with Detroit were not picked up by management.

In 1964, while pitching for the Senators, this once promising major league pitcher went on the disabled list, off the disabled list, and back on again. At times, he said, his arm felt strong but most often it did not. And he received conflicting advice from a variety of sources.

Some of the veteran pitchers told him that if he wanted to stay in baseball he would have to pitch through the pain. A few in the medical profession told him to go on the disabled list and give the arm complete rest. Others said he had tendinitis and could be treated with cortisone shots. A torn rotator cuff was not yet introduced as part of baseball's vernacular. He now believes that is what he had. Today it would be treated with surgery. Back then he was sent home; a casualty of a sore arm.

Dave Tyriver, a 1954 high school graduate, played professional baseball for nine seasons in the Cleveland Indian's organization. In his only major league season in 1962, he was recalled from the Triple A Salt Lake City Bees in August. He pitched in four games all in relief. In minor league baseball, he won 78 games and posted four seasons of ten or more victories.

Larry "Dutch" Rennert played on the same high school and Legion baseball teams with Billy Hoeft. But unlike Hoeft, Rennert's pathway to professional baseball took a different route.

After graduating from Oshkosh High, Rennert headed west where he got into recreation baseball umpiring. His love of baseball and his flamboyant style of calling balls and strikes caught the eye of a former major league umpire who saw talent and convinced him to go to umpire school.

After sixteen long years working in the minor leagues, Dutch got the call to umpire in the National League in 1973. His umpiring career in the majors would last twenty years. During that time he umpired in six National League Championships, two All-Star Games and three World Series.

He was considered one of the game's most colorful and entertaining characters, best known for his animated and loud strike calls. A 1983 *New York Times* poll resulted in his selection as the National League's best umpire.

After 20 years as a major league umpire, Dutch Rennert decided to retire. When asked about his distinctive strike calls behind the plate in an interview in 2015, Rennert said: "You've got to add something to your work. You've got to be a little bit more colorful. But I think I got carried away. But it wasn't an act. It just came natural."

Chapter Nineteen
Bowling

Bowling during the early part of the 20th century was essentially a working-man's sport played in taverns where a few alleys were set up to attract the drinking crowd. As interest in the game expanded it moved away from its saloon origins and gained respectability.

Oshkosh had a number of these tavern-type bowling alleys in the early 1900s. Jerry's Bar, formerly the Wendell Saloon and Bowling Alleys, the oldest tavern in town, had two working bowling lanes up until the end of WWII.

Marty Wesenberg, former owner of Jerry's on Ceape Street, told me there were two bowling alleys attached to the building. "They bowled with a wooden ball about this big," suggesting with his hands that the ball may have been the size of a cantaloupe.

Baumgartner's on North Main Street and Van's Tavern, now Trail's End, each had a couple of alleys during this time as did Freys and Bestlers located on the second block of Main. Street.

Koplitz's, on the corner of 14th and Oregon, had a four lane house and was still operating during the Prohibition era. It became the Acee Deuce during the latter part of WWII when Jimmy Pollnow became the new owner. It was a place many of us started our pin-setting years.

Joseph Dichtl, owner of the Elkhead Bowling Alleys, later known as the Elbow Room, also ran a pair of bowling alleys on Oregon Street as did Richard Rief, later owned by Rudy Novotny inside their tavern on 6th Street.

There were others as well.

Most of those tavern-operated bowling alleys stayed open during the 1920s and '30s when the sales of alcoholic beverages were prohibited. They either were soda parlors and the like or sold illegal beverages on the sly.

When the Hotel Raulf opened in 1927, twelve bowling lanes were built on the ground floor. And as interest in bowling continued to grow more bowling houses were built. St. Mary's soon opened their eight lane establishment as did the Eagles, and the Elk's Club.

With the opening of these new bowling houses the era of the two and four-lane bowling establishments would soon come to an end. The Acee Deuce with its four lanes would continue its operation until the mid-1960s.

In 1939 an eight lane bowling establishment was built in a former Cadillac garage. Expensive cars were no longer selling in the 1930s when Clarence "Gabby" Wirtz and his wife Francis decided to buy the property on South Main Street and proceeded to turn it into the largest south side bowling house.

When the Wirtz couple opened their business in September of 1939 Oshkosh had five bowling establishments: the Eagles, St. Mary's. Acee Deuce, the Raulf Hotel and the Elk's Club, all of which are now closed including the Recreation Bowling Alleys the Wirtz couple opened.

The Recreation Alleys, also known as the "Rec," was located on the east side of South Main Street between seventh and eighth streets across from a building that once was the home of Heiss Bakery.

As bowling became popular with a cross-section of the community, more bowling establishments opened including the T&O, Shoreview Lanes and the Oshkosh Lanes, later named Revs. Revs and the T&O are the only bowling houses still operating in the city.

But there was another bowling establishment built in the 1970s. It was called Spencer Lanes with an unheard of 48 lanes at the time, at least in this part of the state. It was located where Stein's and a few other businesses are now found on the south side of town near Highway 41. It was built on the former site of Well's Department Store, a store similar to a Kmart.

Spencer's, owned by a Chicago businessman, could have, according to some, been the best bowling center in the area. It had the 48 lanes and a recreation area with pool and billiard tables and a number of TV sets in a lounge area located along the west wall of the building. But the problem that Spencer's faced was a large flat roof that leaked when it rained, a roof similar to other bowling houses in the city. The difference was that the owner of Spencer's refused to invest the necessary money to repair the roof. At times, during downpours, pails were placed on some of the lanes to catch the dripping water.

It was up for auction a few years later after the owner filed for bankruptcy. A developer finally bought it and turned it into a mini mall.

Along with a historic glimpse of those bowling lanes constructed over the years I also decided to include one of Oshkosh's top bowlers. He no longer is with us but when bowling was in its heyday, he was one of the best.

In the summer of 2013, Harvey "Hub" Hielsberg, one of the last great bowlers of the 1940s and '50s and the last of the "old-timers" died. He was 100 years old.

His bowling contemporaries may not have been in attendance at his funeral that day but many of us who remembered and bowled with and against this man with his unorthodox style came to show our respects.

I decided while talking to others that there was a story here, a story that needed telling.

After giving it additional thought, I decided to introduce

myself to Karen, one of Hub's daughters. I took her to the side and asked if she would be interested in joining me in an effort to write a story about her father. She said that she and her husband would be happy to do that.

So when I met with Karen and Dennis Haley, a few months later at their home right off Country Club Road south of Oshkosh, I was amazed at what they had to offer.

Hub Hielsberg lived before lane blocking and urethane and resin; a time when bowling national honor counts – a number that seems so modest today – garnered headlines in the sport's section of the local paper. It was a time when the most advanced innovations were a Connie Schwoegler finger-tip and a Pete Kavalski EZ Lift drilled into hard rubber balls that are no longer in use.

The game has changed and so have we and maybe that's the way it should be. But it is still comforting to look back to those Wednesday nights at the Recreation Lanes when the seats were full with spectators and standing room was at a premium.

We came to watch Bireley's, a team comprised of Matt Muza, Rudy Nigl, Bob Putzer, Vic Boeder and Arnie Zuehlke. It was the top team in the city and considered one of the best in the state.

There were others to watch as well as most of the top bowlers in the city bowled on those Wednesday evenings. Names like Eddie Luther, Ed Otto, Augie Fiebig, Marty Ackerman and Paul Priebe rolling those soft roundhouse hooks that were fun to watch in this eight lane establishment. Toppling the pins more with speed than finesse were future Hall of Famers Bill Precour, "Doc" Russell and Carl Genal. "Buster" Thill, "Ducky" Driessen and Dick Zellmer dazzled spectators with their sharp-breaking hooks while brother tandems of "JoJo" and "Porky" Penzenstadler and Jim and Frank Kosup and the upstarts, Harold "Hezzy" Munsch,

Gordy Hielsberg, Louie Draheim and Don Binkowski bring back glimpses of what many called the golden years of bowling.

There were others to be sure. The most notable of those is the subject of this story. His name: Harvey "Hub" Hielsberg.

In 1988 when Hub was 76 his bowling career came to the attention of Joseph Dill, a writer for the *Oshkosh Northwestern.*

With children today taking up bowling almost as soon as they can walk, Hub Hielsberg got a relatively late start in the sport. But he has atoned for that by dedicating a good share of the rest of his life to it.

He got involved with bowling in high school in the late 1920s when he began setting pins at Koplitz's Lanes on the corner of 14th and Oregon. He decided that he liked the game. His first sanctioned average at the age of 20 was 156. Gradually it went up.

His average kept climbing until it peaked at 218 during the 1954-55 bowling season. That was the fourth highest average in the COUNTRY that season. He would also set a city record that year with eleven sanctioned 700s.

It was during that 1954-55 season that Hub received a write-up in the *Milwaukee Journal.* The headline of a story written by Billy Sixty, a *Journal* sport's writer and one of Milwaukee's top bowlers read:

Miller and Hielsberg Hit National Honor Counts.

"Wisconsin's two hottest bowlers, Jimmy "Moe' Miller and Harvey Hielsberg, averaging 220 and 219 respectively, powered their explosive hooks for national honor counts again Wednesday."

"Bowling was a lot tougher in those days," recalled Hielsberg. "The equipment now is a whole lot better and the alleys now are a little bit easier."

Hielsberg has rolled 64 sanctioned 700 series including a 704 at the age of 73 to become the oldest person in Oshkosh ever to top the 700 mark. He has had a league-leading average twenty-two times and was inducted into the Oshkosh Bowling Hall of Fame in 1976.

Hub was the Bowler of the Week at the age of 79 when he rolled a 686.

"I started out with a 258 than had a 279. I ended up with a 149. I'll be 80 in another week and I guess I just slowed down a little that last game."

What I best remember about this quiet and extremely focused bowler during those years we bowled in the same leagues was his unusual bowling attire. Instead of bowling shoes, he wore tennis shoes whose rubber soles occasionally squeaked when he stopped abruptly at the foul line as he delivered his ball to the pocket. I was unaware, as were others, why he chose to wear this unconventional footwear when bowling.

When interviewing Dennis and Karen, Hub's daughter and son-in-law, the two explained it this way.

"He was paranoid about going over the foul line because of his limited vision and the accompanying balance problem he experienced. Hub had only one good eye. Later on he had macular degeneration which further reduced his sight."

"When he was 10 years old he lost sight in his right eye while whittling a piece of wood. Instead of shaving the wood away from his body, he carved away and a piece of that wood flew into his eye. He was at home at the time and his mother pulled the sliver of wood out but he would eventually lose sight in that eye."

Dennis told me about the time he and his father-in-law went down to the Shoreview Bowling Lanes.

"He knew he was old and getting weak and he said

something about the foul line that he wasn't going to embarrass the game by continuing. He thought he could no longer play the game at a respectable level and it was time."

So at the age of 92 he walked away from the sport he loved.

Hub grew up on 9th Street on Oshkosh's south side and attended Jefferson School as a kid. He wanted to be a pharmacist but this was during the Great Depression. He, like many during these hard times, was forced to go to work.

He worked at Morgan Doors for fifty years.

Hub had hernia surgery a year or two after he retired from the game he loved and was sent to an assisted living place to mend and heal. It was soon determined that he couldn't go back and live on his own so the last six or seven years of his life he lived at Park View Health Center.

Dennis told me about this episode during his stay at Park View.

"At Park View when I began reading a story from one of your books, I would pause and he would start talking about the story. He talked about things in the book, the people, the taverns, the stores and businesses you had mentioned and he would talk about them. He grew up in Oshkosh and knew things that many of us did not know."

Karen said that her dad sang all the time even while at Park View.

"As he laid in the Emergency Room of the hospital with a broken hip at the age of 97, he started to sing, 'I fell into a Burning Ring of Fire.' After surgery when the nurse said that she might be driving him crazy with all of her efforts adjusting the devices and weights to make him comfortable, Hub, after hearing the word crazy began singing Patsy Cline's 'Crazy for Losing You.' Every word seemed to remind him of a song. And when he sang in Park View's Christmas Program as part of the cast, it reminded me of the music programs I was involved in during my school years when Dad came to see me."

"He told me it hasn't been easy making it to 100."

"The last words he uttered was to thank the nurses and his family who were gathered at his bedside when he died. He was very gentle, never yelled or swore, was never cross with his children and adored his grandchildren. We miss him so much."

And so do we.

Chapter Twenty
Lakeshore Golf Course

In 2017, the Lakeshore Golf Course considered one of the best public courses in the state was no more. It was sold to the city for the future home of the Oshkosh Corporation. The selling of this historic course still reverberates among those who treasured the course.

The land on which this municipal course was built had previously been owned by Edgar Sawyer. In 1899 Sawyer leased the land to the Algoma Country Club and the club opened a nine hole course. Several years later the members decided they wanted an 18 hole course but the land available at the site was low and marshy so the club decided to relocate.

In 1916 the Algoma Country Club moved south of town where they built the first nine holes and renamed it the Oshkosh Country Club. Six years later they added the second nine.

The Algoma Country Club Golf Course in the meantime went unattended. But there were a few in Oshkosh who believed the city should have a municipal course that everyone could have access to. With this in mind the group appealed to the elected representatives of the city.

In a series of negotiations, Sawyer agreed to trade the park land on the corner of Oshkosh Avenue and Puhoqua Street that bounded Sawyer Creek to the city if the city would name the new land the Mary Jewell Park and later the Mary Jewell Golf Course.

Mary Jewell was Sawyer's wife.

The matter of converting this grazed-out land into a golf

course was then given to the Park Board. The Board said they would consider a public course if there was true interest in the community. But the Board also said that if the group wanted a public course they would have to raise the necessary money to build it.

The group assessed the situation and thought $600 was enough to build the course. They came up with a plan, find 120 men who would pay $5 for the right to play the course the first year at no charge. A golf course was soon resurrected on city land.

To find out how Hank Dettlaff became the first manager and caretaker of this new golf course, I was put in contact with his son, Billy who at the time lived in Florida.

He wrote and said the following story was told to me by my cousin.

"Your dad played a golf match against another guy on Memorial Day in 1921 and the winner would get the job as manager of the new golf course. Hank won the match and was given the job. He was told to have the course ready for a July 4th opening."

The course opened on the same layout as the Algoma Country Club but without greens. Hank Dettlaff, with a short deadline ahead, had his hands full just cutting the grass, getting rid of the weeds and building very informal tees and greens. Each year he would design and build a new green until he had nine of them.

The *Oshkosh Northwestern* wrote of the grand opening in their July 6th edition:

"The opening of the municipal golf links at the Mary Jewell Sawyer Park on West Algoma Sunday was marked by a good attendance. There were about thirty-five persons present, nearly all of whom were novices of the game. Henry Dettlaff, employed as instructor, showed the people how the game is played the proper way as he addressed those present. For those who had never played the game and had no outfit, clubs were provided, there being ten sets purchased for that purpose."

"On Monday the attendance was also good, although not as large a number that attempted the game on Sunday, but several of them were repeaters. The links have been put into good shape and the course has been lengthened. Under the old Algoma Country Club management, the course was about 2765 yards in length. It is now 2971 yards."

One of the important stories in the history of Lakeshore occurred when the Revolta family relocated from Omro to Oshkosh in 1923 and purchased a home just south of Oshkosh Avenue. Johnny Revolta was 12 at the time.

Revolta told Billy Dettlaff this story when he visited him in Evanston, Illinois, when Revolta was the club professional there.

"I was upstairs in my bedroom one morning and happened to be looking out the window and saw these people walking with sticks in their hands. I wanted to know what was going on so I walked up the road to the clubhouse and asked your father what those people were doing. He said they were playing golf and asked if I would like to try."

"Johnny started to play, practiced a lot, fell in love with the game and had the kind of personality that when he liked something, he just threw himself into it. In 1925 at the age of 14, he played in the Wisconsin Caddy Tournament at Grand Park in Milwaukee and won the State Caddy Championship."

"He became my father's caddy master and in 1927 was hired as the assistant professional at the club. My father made him his own personal caddy and took him to all the tournaments as a playing partner."

"Revolta had a friendship at the time with David Rose who

was the golf pro at the Oshkosh Country Club. He went with Rose, who had formerly been a Scottish professional, to Florida during the winter where he continued to work on his game. He came back to Wisconsin and starting winning tournaments including the Wisconsin State Open Championship as a 19 year old. He took a job the following year at a club in Menomonee, Michigan and a year later was the golf professional at the Tripoli Course in Milwaukee where he again was able to compete in the Wisconsin Open."

Revolta turned professional in 1933 and played against the finest golfers of the day and finished as the top money winner in the country in 1935.

It is worth noting that the Oshkosh Municipal Golf Course is – or I should say was - a historic place because it was one of the first municipal golf courses in the country. Most golf courses in the 1920s were private bastions of the wealthy. But thanks in part to President Franklin Delano Roosevelt, who, perhaps inadvertently, made golf available to the masses.

In the 1930s FDR wanted to put people back to work with his New Deal programs. The city of Oshkosh was fortunate to win funds from a few of these programs to provide jobs for some of the city's unemployed. The city also sent an application to the Work Progress Administration (WPA) for money to help expand the course.

The WPA was a New Deal program designed to help stimulate the economy. The country was in the midst of the worst economic depression in its history and President Roosevelt's Administration thought one way to put the country back on a firm financial footing was to provide jobs for the unemployed. The program accepted the city's request for funds to expand the course to 18 holes, and also provided additional dollars to build a clubhouse which stood until it was replaced some fifty years later.

The 18 hole course was opened on Memorial Day in 1936. It would become known as one of the finest public courses in Wisconsin and is the only municipal course to host the Wisconsin PGA Sectional Championship. It was hosted by Lakeshore in the late 1930s, at least in part, to honor Hank Dettlaff's tenure in Wisconsin golf.

The *Oshkosh Northwestern* reported that the opening of the second nine holes of the municipal golf course at Mary Jewell Park for play had been announced for Memorial Day.

"The course is in good condition and is expected to attract a large number of sport's fans for the double holiday, Saturday and Sunday," the *Oshkosh Northwestern* reported.

The original Lakeshore Club House

"The double holiday will also see golfers on the other courses – Oshkosh Country Club and Maxcy's. All of the courses are said to be in fine condition and are being played upon by large number of golfers. The sport this year appears to have more devotees than ever before."

The Macy 18 hole course would close in the late 1930s. The course was centrally located in what is now the Red Arrow Park and extended from the present location of the West High School swimming pool to the old K-Mart parking lot. There would not be another Oshkosh public links course until Far Vu opened in the 1960s.

In a matter of a few years Lakeshore would have marked its 100th Anniversary. It is perplexing and more than a bit incomprehensible that the course Hank Dettlaff turned from a virtual hayfield into one of the most beautiful public courses in the state will no longer be the place where countless more teenagers might learn the game that many of their predecessors came to love.

The Lakeshore Golf Course is now part of our history. The city sold more than thirty acres of the course to Oshkosh Truck, a defense contractor and a major employer in the city. The disposal of the remaining seventy acres of this course, that was once considered the finest municipal course in the state, will be developed into a park.

Chapter Twenty-One
Polio

*I*n many respects the polio outbreak of the 1950s was symbolic of the age. The fear of nuclear war and communism paralleled with polio as the nation's three biggest fears. Americans were afraid of polio and the bomb and they tended to think of them in the same terms as sudden forces that would attack without warning and destroy their own and their children's lives.

Until the vaccine became available, parents lived in fear and hoped their child would not be the next to contact polio. Mothers kept their children in the yard, away from communal outdoor activities, and, more importantly, away from strangers.

Isolation and quarantines were common practices. You didn't go to a lot of group things – parks, swimming pools, other public places - because the authorities weren't sure how the disease spread. We were told to avoid as much person-to-person contact as possible.

Most everyone who grew up in the early 1950s recognized the symptoms: sore throat, difficulty swallowing, headache, slight fever, occasional vomiting and simply feeling sickly. Because the cause of polio was unknown, people searched for answers and blamed many things. Some thought flies and mosquitoes caused polio. So a number of cities, including Oshkosh, fogged the streets with DDT in hopes of eradicating insects and in turn polio, not knowing the detrimental effect this chemical would cause.

These past few years the Coronavirus epidemic sparked a culture war with people arguing over face masks and social distancing. By contrast during the 1940s and '50s, Americans formed a united front against polio. President Franklin Delano Roosevelt, who was felled with polio at the age of 39, encouraged ordinary citizens to donate their spare change to polio research through the March of Dimes. Millions, from all walks of life, answered the call.

In 1955 Wisconsinites saw the worst polio epidemic in state history.

Although the Salk vaccine would become effective in April, Wisconsin reported 921 cases and 134 deaths due to polio by August. The Fox Valley had more polio cases per population than anywhere in the country. Residents quarantined their children, canceled public events and gave money to the March of Dimes. The March of Dimes provided three general duty nurses to the polio ward at Mercy Hospital, and it was equipped with iron lungs for its patients.

One of my friends was struck with polio at the age of 6 in 1939. He was, as the <u>Oshkosh Northwestern</u> in a featured article in February of 2004 stated, the first Oshkosh case of the crippling viral disease that launched an epidemic across America and paralyzed the Fox Valley, making it the polio hot spot in the nation. The disease came out of nowhere and attacked quickly in the 1940s and 1950s.

"It was just like my arm and leg had gone to sleep and I couldn't do anything," Milo Miller said. "No one had any idea where this came from or what caused it. Some thought it came from the common housefly or mosquito."

The polio epidemic stretched over nearly two decades before a vaccine, developed by Jonas Salk, was developed.

This is Milo Miller's story.

It was August of 1939. I was being taken to my grandparent's farm by my mom and dad, Clarence and Viola Miller. They were going to the Beaver Dam County Fair. My uncle, Harvey Baerwald, mentioned to my parents that I wasn't feeling well because I sat on my grandmother's lap most of the day. Otherwise I would have been outside getting into some kind of mischief.

We went home that night and the next morning I could not move my right arm or leg. Our family doctor at the time was Dr. Henry Romberg. He called in several other doctors to examine me and it was decided that I had polio. They had no idea what caused it. They really did not know anything about it because I was the first case in the city of Oshkosh.

We were quarantined for several weeks. No one could visit because they thought that polio was very contagious. Our food was left on the front steps by the City of Oshkosh Welfare Department. I sure got tired of rice, oatmeal and chipped beef.

During the time I was homebound I wasn't able to walk for over a year. A teacher was brought in some months into the quarantine and kept me up with the basic subjects. I was originally right-handed but because of the paralysis of my right side I had to learn to use the left hand. When I first began writing with my left hand I made my 3s and 9s backwards. Eventually the teacher got me squared away.

I had attended Smith School before all this happened and everything that I had come in contact with at school was burned – pencils, paper, desks, books, etc. When I was again allowed back in the public schools about a year or so later, I was sent back to Smith. I was put into an "Open Air Room," a room designated for handicapped kids. We were given a hot meal at noon. The food wasn't bad. A lot of it was government surplus stuff. The worst thing I had to do was take a tablespoon of cod liver oil each day. Bad stuff!!! We could drink our milk with it to go down, but that didn't help much. I made some kid in class laugh after he had taken a spoonful of the nasty stuff and he expelled it and sprayed the teacher. She was not too happy. I had to sit in the corner for punishment. After lunch we would roll out the cots and take a 45 minute nap.

I finished 4th grade at Smith and then was sent to another "Open Air Room" at Roosevelt School. There I finished grades five and six and then went to South Park Junior High to attend regular classes.

When I was about ten, the doctors sent me to the children's Hospital in Madison. It was here that one doctor suggested that growth in my left leg should be cut so that my right leg could catch up in growth. My dad told him to go to hell. He said I had one bad leg and I didn't need another.

On one of those visits I had to stay for more tests. I was there for about two weeks but it seemed like two years. I was put into a room with about ten other boys and I was scared. I walked in my sleep at night. I was told not to do this but apparently I couldn't help it. To solve the problem the nurses tied my right arm to the bed above my head. Then they put several heavy sand bags on my legs. Needless to say this stopped my sleep walking.

I saw boys and girls completely paralyzed, painted in iodine from neck to toes and put in Iron Lungs. These machines helped them breathe. The noise the Iron Lungs made could be heard throughout the hospital.

Before I was released, they put me in a Plaster of Paris cast. This cast covered my entire upper body. My arm was at a right angle and put straight up into the air. I wore this for about three months. It did nothing to help the arm. You need to remember that the doctors knew nothing about polio and how to treat it. Everything was experimental.

After the cast was removed they put my arm into what they called an "Airplane Splint." Why they called it that I don't know. This apparatus was a flexible steel corset that extended from my waist to just under my armpits. It laced up the chest. My arm rested on a leather-padded steel bar that swiveled at the elbow and was held in place by leather straps. I wore this contraption for about three years. It did not help.

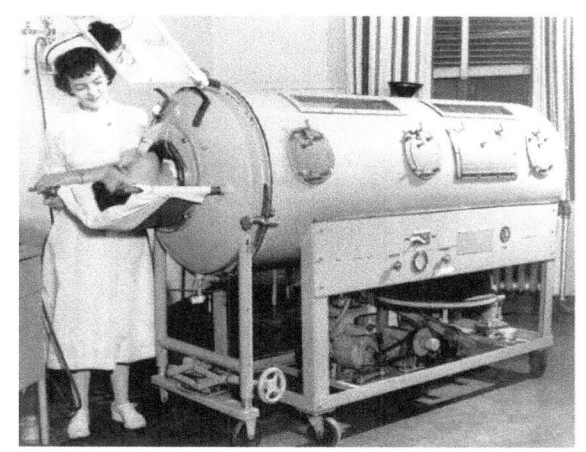

Iron Lung

While I was attending the workshop, they asked if I would like to attend a camp for handicapped boys and girls. It was called "Camp Wawbeek." It was in the Wisconsin Dells area. The camp is still used today. It is supported by the Wisconsin Elks organization with which I have been a member for over 35 years. The Elks have donated thousands of dollars to this camp to help people adjust and improve their lives.

At the camp we took nature hikes, made things in art classes, and did a lot of exercising. It was here that I learned how to swim. I continued at the camp until I was too old to attend.

People today ask me how I learned to do all the things that I can do. I can't give them an answer. You just do what you can. If that doesn't work, you try something else.

You need to have a good attitude, a good sense of humor and a lot of friends. All in all, things have worked out well for me. I consider myself very fortunate to have accomplished what I have.

Chapter Twenty-Two
Highway 41

Highway 41 was originally a two lane highway that ran through Oshkosh on its way to the northern part of the state. It took many hours for travelers to reach their desired destination as many other main streets in cities along the way slowed their journey.

The former route of Highway 41 went through Neenah/Menasha and Appleton and then extended northeast to Little Chute and Kaukauna before arriving in Green Bay.

But it wouldn't be long before there was official talk of rerouting Highway 41 around Oshkosh and those Fox River Valley cities. It would provide an important link from the metropolitan centers of Milwaukee and Chicago with the recreation areas in Wisconsin and also expand business opportunities throughout the state.

It is interesting to note some of the happenings that occurred when the old highways 41 and 45 went through the city.

When I interviewed Gloria Gibson Lennon some years ago about Gibson Motors and Lennon's Grocery Store both located on Main Street, Gloria's daughter, Kathy Lennon, tells this story.

"In the 1920s when Al Capone and his henchmen came through Oshkosh on their way to Eagle River he would, according to the story that made the rounds in our family, invariably stop at Gibson Motors to have his car serviced. Gibson's had one of the very first Cadillac franchises in the state and the only one between Capone's Chicago and his vacation spot in Eagle River."

It has also been said by others that Capone, along with other Chicago mobsters, often drove through town on the old 41 to their retreats to the north woods. I was told that Capone and his boys often stopped for a few drinks at Mary's Bar (next to the Acee Deuce) on Oregon Street before continuing on their journey.

When I questioned why they stopped Mary's Bar, a very small and seemingly unimportant tavern as these Chicago travelers continued on their way up north, I turned to the *Oshkosh Beer Timeline Blogger*, and discovered there may have been a reason they stopped at this small, family owned business. During Prohibition years it housed an illegal commercial brewery in the back part of the building, (the only one on the south side of town) and it operated in tandem with Mary Kollross's speakeasy that faced Oregon Street.

After Prohibition ended in 1933, Mary stayed in the tavern business until sometime in the 1960s when it was purchased by her next-door neighbor, Herb Pollnow of the Acee Deuce for rental purposes.

Each of these stories brings back a time in the 1920s and '30s that connects Oshkosh and surrounding communities to the wider world of illicit booze, prostitution rings and the heyday of Chicago crime.

George Kontos of Butte des Mort told me this during an interview some years ago.

"All travelers had to go by our place (Jimmy's White House in Butte des Mort) before highway 110 was constructed. Dillinger was one of those travelers who stopped to eat a sandwich at Jimmies."

"I remember I was sitting on the cigar display case (he was not yet a teenager) and this tan car parked up alongside the inn. It appeared that the car had a V shaped front like a Ford or Lincoln. There were four in the car. When the car door opened, one stayed back behind the wheel with the car running while the other three entered the inn. One – it could have been

Dillinger – sat down at the counter while the other two moved to other parts of the restaurant; one went towards the kitchen, the other stood near the back of the restaurant. When the man at the counter was done, the three exchanged places until everyone had a chance to grab a bite to eat including the one behind the wheel."

"The man who owned the Mobil Station across the street with his sleeping quarters above the station thought it was Dillinger. He sat up there looking out the window with his 30.06 getting ready to shoot because he thought we were being robbed. Apparently, he had heard that Dillinger had left Chicago and was heading north."

"As soon as the car left the guy from across the street came rushing over and asked if we had been robbed. My grandmother told him that they had just come in, ordered their food and left. In fact, she said one of them told her that he loved her apple pie."

A few days later Dillinger had the well-publicized shootout at Little Bohemia in Manitowish Waters. The shootout gave credence to the story that Dillinger and his men dined in Jimmie's White House before driving north to their hideout in northern Wisconsin.

A new two-lane highway was built in the early 1950s that would eventually replace the old Highway 41.

Lake Butte des Mort's two lane bridge

It was reported in the January 2, 1953 issue of the *Oshkosh Northwestern*: "A two-lane ribbon of concrete stretching north from the south county line to Highway 21 west of Oshkosh was the biggest highway news in Winnebago County in 1952."

"The biggest news in 1953," the paper continues, "is expected to be made by another link in the Superhighway chain – the Lake Butte des Mort Bridge."

By June of 1955 a two-lane Butte des Mort Bridge was completed that extended the new Highway 41 all the way to Green Bay without entering any of the Fox Valley cities. But there was a problem with the bridge. It was built too low to the water and when boats needed to move back and forth from the Fox River to Lake Butte des Mort, traffic on the highway was at a standstill until the boat(s) joined the body of water for which they were headed.

When the additional two lanes were completed in 1967 making it a four lane highway, motorists no longer had to worry about being delayed by boat traffic on Lake Butte des Mort. There now would be a minimum of 30 feet clearance between the bridge and the lake at high water.

But there were still problems not yet resolved on Highway 41. *The Paper* (an Oshkosh newspaper that existed for about three years) in their May 9, 1970 edition stated the following:

Traveling east on 9th Street at the intersection of highway 41 before the overpass was built

"The intersection of highway 41 and Ninth Avenue is earning a bloody reputation."

"Each day, there are 17,000 cars traveling north and south that pass through the four lanes of highway 41. And on Ninth Avenue near the highway, 3,000 cars go east and west on an average day."

"Traffic problems there are getting worse each day as the area continues to be developed. Mushrooming business along the highway, and the new Westhaven subdivision west of it, are creating a traffic tangle. There is no overpass. Construction won't begin on one until at least the summer of 1971."

"During the first quarter of 1970," The Paper continues, "there were five property damage accidents and three personal injuries. Lt. Edward Misch of the department described the intersection as one of the worst in the county."

"Anytime you have an intersection with a four-lane highway, you're going to have accidents," he said, "and this one seems to be especially bad."

"Many drivers on Ninth Avenue apparently got sick of waiting for an opening in the highway traffic. By taking a chance and pulling into the lane of traffic some get hit. Occasionally someone is killed."

"Signs reading 50 miles per hours are posted along highway 41 in the Oshkosh area but having drivers stay within the speed limit is another question. Currently getting from Copps to K-Mart, a car must pull onto Highway 41. Construction of an overpass at Ninth Avenue is expected to start in the summer of 1971."

"In the meantime what should drivers do to prevent accidents at Ninth and 41? "Avoid the intersection," said Misch.

He suggested two alternate routes to get across highway 41 from the Westhaven subdivision. "Take Oakwood Road to K or to highway 21. It's better than taking a chance a 9th and 41, he said.

"State Highway Commission Chairman G. H. Bakke said that Oshkosh cannot expect a vehicle overpass over highway 41 at Ninth Avenue before 1972."

The overpass on 9th Street did begin in 1972 and was eventually replaced with a new overpass with four roundabouts in 2011. The following year roundabouts were constructed on the Highway 21 overpass as well. And there have been many other improvements made over the past number of years as resident of Oshkosh well know.

But the completion of the four-lane Highway 41 and its overpasses in Oshkosh and in other Fox Valley cities had a negative impact as well. These cities soon experienced a loss of retail business on their main commercial arteries.

Main and Oregon streets in Oshkosh soon lost out the dynamic engines of progress. The interstate system of highways that helped accelerate the country's economic growth also had the unintended consequence of slowly strangling these commercial centers to death. The changes came in increments but they came. By the 1980s Main Street, as well as Oregon Street was teetering on the brink of collapse. It was sad to watch.

They are no longer the centers of commerce I once knew. They, long ago, were rerouted to the west.

Chapter Twenty-Three
The New Immigrants

These are not the usual immigrant stories of Germans, English, Irish and other Anglo-Saxon Europeans who arrived in the United States during the 19th and early part of the 20th centuries. The stories you are about to read are immigrants from different cultures, from different parts of the world. They're included here because I knew each of them personally and thought their stories needed telling.

The following story is about a couple who emigrated from Sicily. Faro and Serafina Vitale who owned the best Italian restaurant in the town, offered a menu that drew people from a variety of other places to sample their authentic Italian and Sicilian cuisine.

It was not always easy for this Sicilian couple who moved to Chicago shortly after their marriage. They knew the possibility of future success required hard work, putting money away and a resolve to find their way in their newly adopted country.

I got to know Faro and Serafina Vitale and their two children, Salvatore and Rita, when they opened their first restaurant on Main Street. I was one of many taken in by their cooking.

So when I saw Faro recently at the Saturday Farmers Market I asked if he and his wife would be willing to sit down with me and tell their story.

This is what I learned.

They grew up in a small Sicilian community of Cinisi, a small village some fifteen miles outside of Palermo, the capital. They knew each other growing up, and although they were not related both Serafina and Faro had the same last name.

Like many Sicilian boys during this time, Faro had only three years of formal schooling. He was then expected to help out at home by working at jobs available for young boys. He, like so many others, harvested olives, picked tomatoes and beans, and worked other agricultural-type jobs that young boys were capable of doing.

When he was in his late teens looking for more substantial paying work there was little to be had. The few factories nearby were small and when work was available it would last for just a short period of time.

Seeing little opportunity to better himself in his homeland, Faro in 1965 at the age of 18 went to New York City to find work.

He came with his parents and the three lived in his aunt's apartment. After a short time Faro found a job in a bakery. He was assigned tasks that were tedious and boring. Seeing little opportunity to learn new skills he and his parents went back home after a year.

Faro tells it this way.

"When I was a kid and I was work-ready there was little work there. So I came to this country. It was kind of hard at first. Can't speak English, don't know nothing, worked hard but left after a year."

After a three month stay in his hometown not finding full-time employment, still searching to learn new skills and hoping to find a good paying job he went to Chicago and stayed with a relative who had arrived some years earlier. He soon found a job at the Salerno Cookie Factory.

For fourteen years, following a few months stay in his village, Faro would return to Chicago to work at the cookie factory after not finding what he was looking for back home.

"I work hard, save a little money and then back to Sicily. It was too hard to get a good job so I came to Chicago. I was looking for opportunity. What else could I do?"

Faro married his childhood sweetheart Serafina in 1971. One week later he returned to Chicago to continue to work at Salerno. That's where the work was and he would now need money to support his new family.

He continued at the cookie factory but was always on the lookout for something better. That something came along when he met someone who owned an Italian restaurant.

"I wanted to do something different so I said to this friend that I'll come to work for you. You don't have to pay me. I want to learn the business. I said I'll come when I can and I go when I go."

Faro was now in his md-20s, married with a son and a daughter, still working a ten hour day but not making much money. Serafina, determined to help, found a job that allowed this family of four to pay the bills and put away a little extra.

After working for a year she was told to stay home with the kids.

This is how Faro tells it.

"I wanted my wife to take care the kids. She said she could work and make a little bit of money. I said no. I was a wife and a man. I work enough. When she go to work I had to take care the kids. Although she made a little bit of money I told her, you take care the kids. I work."

The old country had come to America.

Faro worked at the restaurant when he could while holding down a full-time job at Salerno's. Six months after he started, the chef left. The owner realizing he needed help in the kitchen, asked Faro if he would work Friday and Saturday nights, his busy time. If he would, he would teach him what he knew about the food business.

Faro agreed. He was paid $40 a night and together with his pay at Salerno's the two began putting money away, a little bit at a time.

After working at the restaurant for two years, he continued his search for an opportunity to better himself and his family.

Three years later he made a momentous decision.

"I said to my wife, I work so many years and we got so much. If I work so many years there's nothing there. So we're going to take a chance to open a pizza place."

But why Oshkosh?

Serafina said that they came to Wisconsin once a year while they lived in Chicago. They had friends in the Waupun area and during their annual vacation they would visit the surrounding area. When they came to Oshkosh, they liked what they saw.

"We had saved some money but it was not a lot," remembered Serafina. "We could have opened up a pizza store in Chicago but the little bit of money we had we thought our chances were better in a smaller community."

"We rented this small place on Main Street. It was formerly a Mexican restaurant. We cleaned it up, changed it over to an Italian restaurant, named it Tony's Pizza and Italian Restaurant and opened up for business. This was 1980."

For two years they scratched and saved, scratched some more and then business began to pick up. Vitale's was now the place to go.

After more than four years at the Main Street location, the Vitale's realized their restaurant was becoming too small for their business. So they looked around and eventually found it on Murdock Street. They bought the old Sno-Cap Drive-In Restaurant.

Vitale's

They took out the drive-in part of the building and remodeled inside and out. They put in a bar and whatever else needed to make it large enough and welcoming enough for their customers.

Their Main Street customers followed. Other customers came as well. Even from those outside the city.

"We got people from all over the state to eat at our place. We even had people visiting from Chicago, from New York City and other places. They came because they found out we served good food."

Ginger DeShaney wrote this story in the September 16, 1992 issue of the *Northwestern*.

Authenticity.

Plain and simple – that's what sets Vitale's Italian Restaurant apart from others.

"It's guaranteed to be authentic," said owner Faro Vitale.

Vitale is from Sicily so he knows what the real stuff is, he said. "I came from there you know."

When he and his wife Serafina, opened their restaurant in 1980, it was slow to take off. Mrs. Vitale said she doesn't think anyone knew what Italian food was then.

Through word-of-mouth and curiosity, people started flocking to the restaurant.

Mrs. Vitale said people from New York and Chicago have commented that Vitale's sauce is the best they've ever had.

"The sauce and the bread are made from scratch daily," Vitale said. "Our food is always fresh. Every day we experiment with something new."

Their business grew by leaps and bounds and after a few years they no longer needed to advertise. Business was that good.

"Our advertising was basically word-of-mouth. Many said it was the best meal they ever had, the best sauce they ever ate. We were a little surprised when such comments came from people living in big cities."

"Most came in for pasta dishes, not for pizza. They would say we can eat pizza anywhere but no place else serves pasta like you do. It made us feel good."

"We were noted for the veal dishes. I'm careful when I buy the veal. I look for the best cuts. It must be tender and I buy in small quantities. Chicken Faro is another favorite for our customers. It's a dish I experimented with until I get it to taste the way I wanted it."

"I had family recipes. I experimented over the years. Some of the dishes on the menu I would just 'monkey around' until I was satisfied with how it tasted. If it was good, I put it on the menu. Our meals were unique because I experimented. And if customers would continue to ask for it I knew it was good."

"From nothing I built something."

When my daughter worked there I asked what she recommended. "Buy the half-order of baked mostaccioli, you'll have plenty to eat and you'll love it."

I ordered it most every time I was there. And I was there a lot.

After ten successful years they moved to a new location. They moved because Walgreen's wanted to build a new store on the corner of Jackson and Murdock. And they needed to buy the property owned by Nolte's Service Station on the corner and the building occupied by Vitale's Restaurant.

"We negotiated for three years. Each time they made an offer I said it was not enough. So one day they asked what do you want? I knew what it was worth and they finally paid me that amount."

"We bought the land and building across the street. It was a fast food place named Juicy Lucy's. The building was razed and a new restaurant was built."

In a *Northwestern* dining review, Ken Melchert wrote this about Vitale's and their new building.

Sicilian natives Faro and Serafina Vitale have served up Italian fare in several Oshkosh locations since 1980. Vitale's Restaurant recently opened in a beautiful new brick and stucco neo-classical building on the north end of Oshkosh. The quietly elegant design continues inside with pewter chandeliers hanging from vaulted ceilings over deep green carpeting. There is a large bar and party room off to one side.

They stayed in the business for another three years and then sold it to longtime employees Alberlado Lopez and Chad Ewing in 2001.

In the Business section of the *Northwestern* of September 8, 2001, Sean Fitzgerald wrote:

The hospitable smile and strong Sicilian accent of Faro Vitale still graces the dining room of the Oshkosh restaurant that bears his name despite his recently selling the business and moving into semi-retirement.

Vitale 54 turned over the reins of his 21 year-old operation to longtime employees Chad Ewing and Alberlado Lopez this past summer. But the Sicilian immigrant will stick around as an employee for at least two years helping to prepare the breads and family-recipe sauces which have made Vitale's the longest-standing Italian eatery in Oshkosh.

"It will always be Vitale's," Ewing said. "I have a hard time telling people he's not the owner anymore because in my mind he'll always be the owner. He's kind of a mentor. He's kind of a consultant."

Faro stayed around two years helping prepare breads and family recipe sauces and then decided to leave.

How did the new owners do in the business?

"To be successful you have to work hard, put in a lot of hours, oversee things. He didn't always want to do that. He didn't take kindly to advice. After helping them out in the kitchen for two years I felt I wasn't listened to and felt they wanted to do it their way. So I stepped aside."

"He might have thought the business would always be there as it was when he worked for me. He was too concerned with making money."

"I would get up at seven and go to the market always trying to buy local and buying fresh when I owned the restaurant. We didn't freeze anything. He had to sell everything even if it wasn't fresh. In the summer I would buy tomatoes by the bushels and make it into sauce."

"I would buy my meat once a week at Buttman-Binner, a local meat market. They knew I wanted the best quality cuts and because my restaurant trade was similar each week, they knew the type of cuts and the amount I would need each of those weeks."

"The business at the end was not so good," Serafina said. "We're not sure of the reason."

Was the food good?

"Maybe not. It was not the same."

It was also too bad for Faro and Serafina because the place

was still called Vitale's.

"Some people did not know that we no longer owned the business. I'm sure it affected our reputation."

Running out of questions, I asked where could I go if I wanted good Italian food.

Serafina quickly pointed to her kitchen.

She said they never go out, although she did admit later on that they went once to Culver's.

"Even when we go out of town we never, never order Italian food. We know what good Italian food tastes like. I know what's good so I eat at home."

Faro died shortly after the interview. He was only 68. Serafina and her daughter Rita, suffering from his unexpected death and not wanting to write his obituary, asked if I would do it.

The following two stories are of two students I had in history class in the 1980s. The first was born and raised in Turkey but arrived in the United States with an American family who at the time lived in Germany.

To understand her story and the dilemma she faced, I'm including the letter and its attachment I sent to our congressman, Thomas Petri, on October 1, 1984.

The enclosed letter is from one of my current United States history students. About one week ago, Julie asked if she could talk to me about a personal problem. She proceeded to tell me about her alien status and the peculiar restrictions placed on her visa. Because I was unaware of these types of restrictions, I asked her to tell me her story. She did and it is basically contained in the accompanying letter. I was going to correct her word choice, sentence structure and spelling, but decided against it. I felt that any changes would not accurately express Julie's feelings.

Julie so desperately wants to become a naturalized citizen and any efforts you could make in her behalf would be a blessing. I, along with Julie, am asking you to investigate the accuracy, permanency and validity of this visa. If the visa is accurate and valid, our question is:

what can be done to remove the visa restrictions imposed on Julie O'Connell.

My name is Julio O'Connell. That's not my legal name thoe, my real name is Hulya Yagoi and I'm 17 years old. I was born in Turkey. Both my parents are Turkish. When I was younger my parents, me and my two brothers moved to Germany. We were together in Germany for a year.

Then both my parents left my brothers and me within two days. We were send to an orphanage. After 2 years being in an orphanage they told us we had to go back to our home country in Turkey to a Turkish orphanage. We knew how it was to live in Turkey, especially in an orphanage. But at the last moment they found some parents in Sweden, so we were send there for a visite. But those parents were to young for my big brother and me, but they could have keeped my little brother. At that point my brothers and I were going to be separated. They knew that was a bad idea. They knew this family in Germany who were Americans who wanted to adopt kids so we were sent there for a visit. We went back and forth 3 times, and the third time they took us in for good. They did not adopt us, because my natural father did not give the O'Connell's the permission to adopt us.

We lived with the O'Connell family for three years in Germany then decided they wanted to come back to the United States.

After two long years of writing letters to the Congress, the United States gave permission for my brothers and me to enter the U.S. with the O'Connell's. We arrived in Chicago on February 28, 1980.

I now live with different foster-parents here in Oshkosh. This past year I spent a lot of time crying and worrying because there was a 50% chance that I could be sent back to

Turkey. I have come to love this great country of America and accept it as my country. Because I have lived in so many places and traveled a lot I know how people live in other countries and how people are treated – and that there is no greater country then the country of America, a country that is free, a country where your dreams come true.

I love this country and in my heart it is my country but legally I don't belong to this country. But with all my heart I wish I was as lucky as these American kids.

I don't have to worry anymore, wondering if I'm gonna be sent back to Turkey because they found out that I came here under an Humanitarian-Visa. My social worker told me I have a Humanitarian-Visa from the Immigration in Milwaukee which means she said that I am allowed to stay in the U.S. as long as I want to. I am not allowed to become a citizen unless I marry an American.

I would really appreciate it if somebody would please look into it, of how I could become an American citizen. I asked my social worker but all she keeps saying is that the Immigration in Milwaukee says that I can't become a citizen. Please, there must be a way.

I really believe there's a way – maby I'm asking too much and I'm just a big dreamer but I'm going after my dreams. PLEASE HELP ME.

Yours truelly,
Hulya Yagoi (O'Connell)

Congressman Petri responded and stated he would find out what he could do. But before Julie received any information from Immigration, the school year ended and I am unaware of any changes that may have occurred in her status.

This is a story I asked Shoua Yang a Hmong and a *student of mine to write. I asked if she would to put her story down on paper following a talk she gave to my history class.*

A little background is probably necessary to understand Shoua and the Hmong people and their efforts to come to America.

The Hmong were American allies during the Vietnam War. The CIA trained Hmong tribesmen to fight against communist insurgencies in Laos. Under the guidance of the CIA and American Special Forces, the Hmong played critical roles in our war against communist expansion including disrupting the North Vietnamese supply lines on the Ho Chi Minh Trail, providing intelligence about enemy operations, identifying targets for American bombs, and rescuing pilots shot down over Laos.

The United States promised the Hmong people, if we lost the war, that they were welcome to come to America if they thought their lives under communist control might be in danger.

After South Vietnam and its American allies were defeated, the Hmong – men, women and children - were marked for death. They were pursued as they fled by foot and boat swimming for their lives in their attempt to flee their home country. Those lucky enough to survive this traumatic and deadly journey gathered in refugee camps in Thailand.

In 1980, five years after the ending of the war, America reached an agreement with Thailand and passed legislation to allow thousands more of these refugees to settle in the United States. Many settled in the Midwest including Oshkosh and other communities in the Fox River Valley.

This is what Shoua Yang wrote.

1975 came and it was time to run for shelter and freedom. The quicker one runs the better place he will find. So, we moved to a small village consisting less than twenty families. There we lived for two years. My father's mother died and was buried on top of a little hill.

1977 we moved again to another village called Naying. We lived there for less than a year. We were starving, no food was available. My mom and my sister and my brothers were all working very hard in the fields, but they brought no food home. When harvest time came, we couldn't celebrate. Every day they came home exhausted, hurt, and hungry. My mom tried to buy some of our food supplies, but soon we ran out of money.

One morning in 1977, the Vietnamese army caught up with us. They were on both sides of our little village and we were their target. We had less than a day to run for our freedom or surrender. Some surrendered, and some ran for their lives. My family was among those who ran for their lives.

We killed our mother pig, my best pet. She did everything just like a dog pet would do. She was all I had. She was also pregnant at the time she was killed. When some people who had come to our village that morning for shelter, found out that we weren't going to eat the babies, they came to ask for them, the baby pigs. They cooked the babies to prepare for their journeys. I knew it had to be done, but I couldn't look at what was happening to my pet and her premature babies.

That night, we fled back passed the old village into a very deep stream. We spent the night there. It was that night that a family was killed by a huge tree which was struck by the storm. The father died immediately, but the mother was given some opium to end her sufferings. Her breast was split into two parts and her head was partially opened.

The mom and dad died leaving the children behind. The oldest girl, a little girl, a baby, a boy who had a broken leg when this mom and dad died were the survivors. The oldest girl was no older than the age of ten. She offered her baby sister to anyone who would take the baby and along with the baby she offered three cups of salt, which was all she had with her. One of the ladies breast-fed her to quiet her down.

As far as I know I never knew what happened to the baby after her relatives sold her to a couple that didn't have any kids. The poor children were all separated.

The next day, our guards warned us that the Vietnamese had come very close and we needed to move as soon as possible. Everyone started to hide under logs, behind trees and bushes. Later that day we got separated from my uncle, KaGe Hang, and his family because we could not agree on which way to go. The next thing I knew, we were with a man and his family. He and my mom knew each other. His last name was the same as my mom's maiden name. He said if we would follow him he would lead us in Thailand which is where we were trying to escape to. Thailand was our dream land, rich and safe. So, we followed him to a corn field where we stayed the night.

The corn was ready to be harvested, but we found out they, the owners, didn't have a chance to harvest anything they had planted. We ate the corn and the squash for supper.

Morning came and he decided he didn't want us to go with him. He said that he could only take us if our relatives promised not to want us back. My so-called uncle, Noog Vang, said that it could not be done. So, he took us to where our so-called uncle was staying. Uncle Noog Vang decided not to take anyone who could not run, obviously that meant my mom and all ladies with children, like myself, and the old people. He wanted us to surrender. He said he would come back for us as soon as he was in a safe place. So, we agreed to stay.

We walked into an old town. We sat there to wait for the Vietnamese soldiers. The soldiers soon came with a Hmong man marching in front of the soldiers. The man was translating to us not to lie to the soldiers or they will kill us. I was so frightened, tears started to fall down my cheeks. My mom quickly wiped them off. She said that if I cried the soldiers would find out where my brothers were.

Before we started our journey to the camp, my cousin, Chia (Uncle Kade's daughter) had decided to surrender thinking that her parents had already surrendered. Chia said that they had been shot by the soldiers early that same morning.

The soldiers took us to two different places past our village, Nayhing. We ate the food that was given to us by the Vietnamese. We couldn't find any place we wanted to stay in the area. We had to build our own tent to live. Together, my cousin, my mom, and I made our tent and that was our home.

We were moving from place to place. Little girls were being raped by the soldiers. I remember running away from them. I was among the lucky ones who didn't get raped or killed. Everyone else was slave to the soldiers. They, the soldiers, also ate dogs.

My mom worked very hard to get us out of the town. She found someone at last who wanted to go the same way we wanted to go.

We left for our long journey back to the first village that we stayed in. We stayed there for a while, then we moved on. The man that was leading us made my mom and I pay him and his family everything we had, and when we ran out of things to give him he threatened to kill my mom if she doesn't give the opium she had with her.

Moving back and forth was all he ever made us do. He wasn't taking us to my brothers and sister. He didn't even know the way. We didn't have anything to eat. Our starvation began once more. We got to the point where no one could take it anymore. Then he finally gave up. He was taking us to Thailand, our dream land. We weren't sure about it, but he said that our relatives were in Thailand already.

Hoping to see my brothers and sister in Thailand, we were on our way there. A month of walking on bare feet. Some died on the way, some never was able to cross the river, Mekong, the border of Thailand and Laos. My mom and I was among the lucky ones to reach Thailand. We used bamboos to cross the river. We didn't know how to swim. My mom paid a man with her silver necklace, a gift from her mother.

In Thailand we didn't have enough food to last us through the day. We had to work for the Thai government. The Thai government gave us very little food to eat, and if we had no ID we get no food.

Two months after we arrived in Thailand, we registered for a visa with my sister and her family. Our application was approved in mid-June. We took the bus to a camp where we waited for our plane schedule.

Finally, it was time for us to get to the plane. We rode the bus to the airport for our first plane on July, 1980. We were amazed how everything was built at the airport, such as the bathroom, stair ways, escalators, even the building itself. When my mom saw an American woman get on the escalator, she said, "No wonder Americans don't get old too easily, they don't walk much." We took three planes to get to America. We eventually landed in Chicago.

I couldn't speak English at all, so I couldn't say hi to her. A little girl in my sister's family knew how to say hi and someone else knew how to say yes and no. I felt real low. I thought I would never speak as well as they would. I never knew adults had to be educated even though they were old.

Shoua and her family eventually moved to Oshkosh and she and her siblings attended the public schools and adjusted as well to "American ways" as they were able to.

She writes in her last paragraph, "For the next eleven years, I plan to go to college after high school. So, why for so long. My past had been a disaster, but I still have the future in my hand. I care about education of course, I never had it. I didn't have the chance to go to school in Laos. I was a girl."

Chapter Twenty-Four
The Mayor of South Park – The story of Donnie Weitz

It's difficult to write about our past without including those who helped change the historic landscape of our city. One of the most loved and cherished of the many whose contributions helped define our history, is the subject of this story.

He was a south side celebrity, a super star of sorts, a boy creature who was loved and admired by so many. He was a fixture at South Park for years and could be seen roaming the streets of the south side saying hi to most anyone passing his way. He especially loved children and was protective of any child he thought was mistreated or neglected.

Donnie was the first of six children born to Conrad and Dorothy Weitz. When the parents were told about Donnie's retardation, they were devastated. The doctors said that there wasn't much they could do, that Donnie would die young or could live to a ripe-old age.

Donnie was born in 1930 and grew up during a time when programs for retarded children did not exist. So he never attended school. But he wanted to and felt bad that he couldn't. To compensate, Donnie could be seen standing on the corner watching the kids get out of school at South Park and was often seen helping the crossing guards escort school-aged children across the street at the end of the school day.

When I was asked to do a story on Donnie, I didn't know where to turn, who to talk to. Like most south siders, I knew Donnie, saw him countless times at South Park and marching in the Ohio Street Parade but didn't know enough about him to do justice to a story.

Not knowing where to turn first, I decided to send letters to a number of people I knew who grew up in the same neighborhood as Donnie. A few days later, Nancy Veith Drexler called and put me in contact with Jeanne Rasmussen, Donnie's sister. I called Jeanne and told her what I had in mind. She recommended that I write a letter to the editor of the <u>Northwestern</u> asking those who knew Donnie to contact me. She said if you get a fraction of the stories people told at

Donnie's funeral you would have a good start on a story.

Jeanne was right. At least a dozen people wrote or called. Their remembrances allowed me to understand the intimate connection Donnie had with others. But it wasn't until I met with Nancy Drexler, her sister Sally, and her husband Frank at their home one afternoon, and with Jeanne Rasmussen the following morning, that I felt I had the stuff to begin putting the story together.

While I was writing, Larry Muehrer, who had intended to write a book on Donnie a few years back, gave me some of the material he still had in his files. I am truly indebted to all who wrote and called.

This is what I found after interviewing Donnie's sister's Jeanne and from the letters and calls I received.

Jeanne Rasmussen said she never saw her older brother as retarded. He was simply Donnie to her. She said that Donnie had a mind of a 5 year-old but was smart in many ways.

"Donnie always had two wallets, the one in the left front pocket was always empty, the one in the right front pocket is where he stashed his cash. When he was approached by someone he knew and occasionally by people he didn't, he would show that person his empty wallet and invariably receive a small cash gift. As soon as the person was out of sight he would transfer the money to the wallet in his right front pocket and begin anew."

Jeanne talks about one Halloween.

"After Donnie went trick or treating on Halloween a number of times; Donnie, always the thinker, decided to increase his stash of candy by using a pillow case instead of the conventional paper bag. He went house to house trick or treating with a white pillowcase and a smile on his face."

Donnie lived with his sister, Joyce Brown, after his parents died. Rose Scherck, 92, told me over the telephone that "Donnie was over by me all the time when he lived on 5th Street. If I was shoveling snow he would come over and tell me 'Rose, you work too hard.' He always wanted to talk.

Oftentimes I would invite him into the house and we'd have coffee and a couple of donuts or a pop and he always thanked me profusely. When I would give him a couple of dollars for shoveling or something else he was so thankful. He was just a nice man, a kindly person. He always wore a smile."

"Donnie had a sharp mind. He knew people and could rattle off their names. Give his sister credit. He was always neat and clean when he left with his lunch bucket as an 'employee' of South Park grounds crew. Park employees treated him with respect and loving care like a fellow employee."

"I used to live on 6th Street with my parents," wrote Jenny Hopp, "and Donnie would always come past my house and talk to me, giving me a hug and candy. I had a friend with me and he always thought she was my baby sister. It is sad that he is no longer with us. He was one of the good guys in the city of Oshkosh."

Michael Watkins who lived on 9th Street wrote: "Despite Donnie's disability there was a certain dignity about him. He was somewhat aloof and alone yet he always seemed happy and upbeat and would often skip as he walked. While waiting at corners for traffic, Donnie would place the palms of his hands on the back of his head and flap his arms forward back and forth."

Michael mentioned that they had a view out their living room window of the people walking on Ohio Street. When they saw Donnie he was usually carrying a lunch bucket or a sandwich bag as he made the trek to the maintenance building in South Park.

"Donnie was an unofficial park tender. The men working in the park building would give Donnie minor tasks to perform and he would hang out with them. Whatever his role, Donnie took it very seriously as he showed up there every day as if it were a job. The South Park playground was a favorite haunt of Donnie's and you might find him there sometimes with his family on weekends."

"South Park was his home away from home even in his younger years," Mary Brown Laipple, who now resides in Oshkosh four months of the year and in Florida the other eight, wrote:

"During the summer of 1951-52 I had a summer job working for the Oshkosh Department of Parks and Recreation under the direction of Jim Bruins. I was assigned to South Park as a playground director. How great it was to be greeted every day by Donnie Weitz who asked, 'How are you doing today, and is your boyfriend treating you okay?' He loved being there, and many times chose to watch rather than participate in the craft projects, but always asked if he could help me watch the small children in the wading pool. He treated the children kindly, and for the most part, got along very well with everyone."

"After getting married my husband and I spent most of our life in Park Forest, Illinois. Several times a year we would come with our family to Oshkosh to visit friends and family. On occasion I would stop at South Park to see Donnie and was always warmly greeted. When he found out I was married he always asked me, "Is your husband treating you okay?"

One day at South Park, Donnie saw a mother and daughter on the playground. The daughter was fooling around on a piece of playground equipment so the mother scolded the daughter and warned her not to do that again. Donnie, observing all of this, came over and told the mother that she should be nicer to the little girl. "He was," according to this observer, "always sensitive to any perceived mistreatment of others."

Neil Starke was a fireman at the 10th and Ohio Street Station and told me that he saw Donnie most every morning walking proudly from his 5th Street home to South Park carrying his lunch bucket for work as a maintenance worker.

"South Park was a place where you could pump well water that was cool, clean and delicious. When Donnie saw people in line at the pump, he would take over and pump water for everyone."

"When Donnie passed the fire station, he would sometimes stop and talk to the guys sitting outside. One of the firemen that often talked to Donnie was another man by the name Neil. When Donnie found out Neil was hospitalized because of a fire at the Badger Lumber Company he stopped and asked about him. When we explained what happened, Donnie got down on his knees and began praying for Neil's recovery. While he was on his knees praying our fire house got a call telling us another fireman was injured in a fire. Donnie, once again, got down on his knees to pray."

Joe Williamson, who worked at South Park as a pool attendant for the wading pool during the summer of 1969-72 wrote, "As most people know, Donnie was a fixture for many years at the park. The park superintendent at the time, Herman Ristow and his staff really looked after Donnie. Donnie would join them for lunch every day as if were one of the workers. Thinking back, I find it amazing how independent and happy Donnie was by simply being able to enjoy the surroundings of the park. This was his universe and it seemed to suit him just fine."

Jack Steinert who lived a few blocks from the park said, "When our kids were small we would take them to South Park to play on the swings. Donnie would usually be there and he would ask if he could push the kids in the swings. He always said, 'I'll be careful with them' and he was."

Another of his hangouts was the Piggly Wiggly store on Ohio Street. Cliff Sebora, the owner of the store, told his help that if Donnie came in with a quarter and wanted to buy more than a quarter's worth of treats, let him do it. Donnie soon came to understand the value of a quarter at the "Pig" as some called it. One day when he went in to the store, a new and a very young employee was working who evidently was not told of the owner's decree. When Donnie put down his quarter for the usual haul of a Twinkie, a Pepsi, and a variety of candy, he was told that his quarter was not enough. He stormed out of the store not understanding why he was being mistreated.

Jack Steinert said that the family used to shop at Sebora's Piggly Wiggly. "More often than not, when we checked out Donnie would be standing at the end of the checkout line with a Pepsi cola tucked under his arm. His saying was always the same. 'There she is spending all your hard earned money again.'"

Phyllis Johnson, a retired elementary teacher from Franklin School, remembers this about Donnie.

"When I was old enough to go to South Park by myself, I remember Donnie carrying his black lunch bucket every day of the week except Sundays. He would help the two men who took care of the park. He rode along with them on the tractor wagon and did his darndest to help them. They were so good to him, letting him help and feel the self-worth of doing a job well. When the men went home so did Donnie."

"Donnie often talked to us kids too. This is how he got to know me so well and when I was old enough I got a job at Piggly Wiggly across from the park. Donnie never forgot anything I told him about my family or about myself. When I married, he always asked how Carl was doing at work and wanted to know if he made a lot of money at Universal Foundry. He then would always ask me about my sisters and brother and my parents. He NEVER forgot our names, where we worked or the names of our children. Some years after I graduated from college I would see Donnie on occasions and he still remembered everything from those earlier years. He always asked the same questions about the same people. But he remembered."

When I asked my brother, Ray La Point, what he remembered about Donnie, he said: "I had a vague, special awareness of the name and the fact that I should know the guy, but nothing of substance came through. Then when your book appeared on the internet I began reading the chapter on Donnie. Slowly the image formed and then he became three dimensional and I was transported back to the past."

"I could clearly hear his distinct, nasal twang and see his arms flapping and dancing down the street and I was in junior high school again. I was there with him in the park. He was always walking and talking to himself or any others who would listen. I pitied him at times and then pitied myself for thinking I was somewhat better. I learned cynicism; he always saw the best in people."

"My memories of people like Marty Anderson and Donnie Wetiz, unique but as unlike as two people can get, illustrates that it is not necessarily the qualities of people that is so important, but the qualities they bring forth in others. Donnie was no less a teacher than "Coach."

"For many of us," Jack Steinert recalls, 'Donnie was best known for being the Grand Marshall of the Ohio Street Children's Parade. You could always tell when the Ohio Street Children's Parade was about two weeks away. That was when you would see Donnie practicing marching on the sidewalk heading down Ohio to South Park. On parade day almost everyone looked to see where Donnie was marching."

Because Donnie was a fixture on Ohio Street and at South Park, he became the Parade Marshall for the annual Children's Parade sponsored by the Ohio Street Civic Association. He led the parade wearing a huge smile, a WWII helmet liner and carrying a baton that he waved continuously back and forth. Later on after he resided at Park View and could no longer walk the distance, he rode in a car as Grand Marshall. Donnie was, according to both Jack Steinert and Rose Schenck, THE OHIO STREET PARADE.

Donnie Weitz and the Children's Parade

In the winter of 1981 when Donnie was walking down Oregon Street near Mueller Potter drug Store, he was accosted by a man who punched him in the face. It was a blow that broke his nose and gave him two black eyes. Rick Sebora, manager of Piggly Wiggly said, "I know Donnie wouldn't know how to pick a fight. I've seen nothing but kindness from him."

Shortly after the incident, Peggy Bostwick wrote a letter to the editor of our local paper.

"I grew up with Donnie. He was always around to help others and even though some adults and kids laughed at him because of his retardation, he just kept on being enjoyable.

After I married I took my children to South Park often, and here would be Donnie. He always helped me with my kids. Donnie always asked me even after they had grown how they were. The reason this hurts so much is because I too had a retarded brother who was picked on, made a fool of in many ways."

In the summer of 1996 as story appeared in the <u>Northwestern</u> entitled, *A Familiar Face is Missed at South Park.*

"One of Oshkosh's most recognizable people is no longer making his usual rounds at South Park. Sixty-five-year-old Donnie Weitz, who usually carried a lunch pail on his travels, now resides at Park View Health Center. Weitz is especially missed by city employees who have grown fond of him over the years.

Donnie Weitz passed away in 2004 at the age of 73. His life filled with love and compassion had not gone unnoticed.

Shortly after Donnie died, Brian Poeschl, a member of the Oshkosh Common Council, suggested that the asphalt road winding through South Park be named Weitz Lane in honor of Donnie. Poeschl said the idea came from Richard Binder, an Oshkosh resident. "Donnie was a landmark. He was quite a fellow all the way around. Joyce Brown said her brother would be honored to have a road in South Park in his name. "Nobody in our family is a celebrity like him and he didn't even try."

Unfortunately for the Weitz family and especially for the Oshkosh community, it never passed muster with the Council.

John Baier, of Edmond, Oklahoma, said it best. In a letter to the *Oshkosh Northwestern* shortly after Donnie passed away, he wrote.

"As a native and longtime south side resident, I was saddened to read the news of Donnie Weitz. As a child playing at South Park, he represented the first developmentally disabled person I had met. Through the wisdom of my parents, Donnie became an 'OK person' and my first lesson in understanding and acceptance of special people like him. That lesson learned in South Park has served me well throughout my life. Although I've been away for more than 15 years, Oshkosh will always be home for me. Upon seeing the dedication to Donnie Weitz at the playground at South Park during our annual visit this past July, I couldn't help but feel proud to be from a place where such a special person became such an important part of the community.

About the Author

Ron La Point is a retired high school history teacher. Since his retirement, he has written eight books on the history and people of Oshkosh including his latest: Oshkosh Remembered.

Printed in the USA
CPSIA information can be obtained
at www.ICGtesting.com
LVHW091411140624
783242LV00029B/335